The Covid-19 pandemic revealed just how much fear can grip the world. From the lowest to the highest levels of society, we saw an entire generation paralyzed. But now Mark Filkey has provided a roadmap to show us the way out of fear. His book is important not only for this moment in our culture but also beyond. Mark is exactly right that Fear Must Not Win—especially when it comes to Christian believers. If you've struggled with fear at any level, this book is for you. Win back the confidence that God has provided for us and step back out with the courage to change the world.

—*Phil Cooke, PhD*
Author, *The Way Back: How Christians Blew Our Credibility and How We Get It Back*

In his latest literary installment, Bishop Mark Filkey tackles what I'm convinced is the greatest enemy we all face: FEAR. The primary theme threaded throughout the pages of *Fear Must Not Win* is how to deconstruct and destroy the fears in your life that are holding you back from your very best self. With delightful and thoughtful prose, Bishop Filkey coalesces rich theology, powerful revelation, and practical experiences to help the reader form strategies to fight back against fear. Fear must not win, and this marvelous read will show you how to make fear lose forever.

—*Pastor Jason Sides*
Christian World Ministries Inc., San Antonio, TX

Far too often, the church in America is only like a visitor center. It's safe, it's warm, and it's comfortable. But we're missing the power of Jesus, the presence of Jesus, and the excitement of following Jesus because we're playing it *safe*! The American "trinity" is comfort, pleasure, and success. And one of our biggest idols is safety. Consequently, we don't want to talk about or face our fears. Preachers often ask, "If you died tonight, do you know where you're going?" I think Jesus would ask a different question: "What if you *don't* die tonight—how are you going to live tomorrow?" In *Fear Must Not Win*, Pastor Mark Filkey does a brilliant job of addressing these issues, helping believers to escape the prison of fear and walk in their God-given victory. Read this book and let Pastor Mark help you beat—*defeat*—the scared inside you!

—*Pastor Rick Godwin*
Summit Church, San Antonio, TX

Bishop Mark Filkey is one of those rare authors who addresses difficult life issues in a practical format while offering profound and relevant insights into *how* to overcome them. *Fear Must Not Win* fully deals with *fear*: it defines it, exposes it, confronts it, and offers us truths to rise above it. Bishop Filkey identifies the origins of people's fear and anxiety and provides real answers. This book is therapy on paper. Thank you, Bishop, for not sidestepping topics that must be addressed. *Fear Must Not Win* is a must-read for those who desire to overcome fear. It's also a tremendous resource for pastors, parents, and leaders who are helping others to overcome it. Fear must not win!

—*Bishop Gary McIntosh*
Founder, Transformation Church, Tulsa, OK

Mark Filkey is a voice of courage and authority in a day when those qualities are needed most. His prophetic insight pierces through the walls of resistance and calls for men and women to rise in our darkest days and step into the Light of promise and purpose. If you focus for very long on news reports or social media platforms, you might find yourself immersed in the fear that our best days are in the past and our positive destiny is quickly dissipating. Some people cry out, "Come quickly, Lord Jesus, and rescue us from this impossible situation!" Not so with prophet-bishop Mark Filkey.

When so many are saying, "Run and hide," Mark rises to the occasion with fire in his eyes, declaring, "It's time to march forth and recover all for the King and His kingdom!" His book *Fear Must Not Win* is a clarion call to never surrender! FEAR MUST NOT WIN! Jesus is still the answer to every question you'll ever ask. And Mark Filkey has the keen ability to hear the voice of God and the courage to declare what he hears. This book is proof. I encourage you to read it as fast as you can and then read it again.

—*David Binion*
Pastor, Dwell Church, Allen, TX
Praise and worship artist

Mark Filkey is a great minister of the Word of God. In his new book, *Fear Must Not Win*, Mark does a tremendous job of walking us through great steps of faith against fear. Fear is a liar, and the devil has no place in our lives as children of God. Take this opportunity to feed your faith with these great testimonies and watch how God will make a way where there seems to be no way. You will be blessed and strengthened by Mark Filkey and *Fear Must Not Win*.

—*Mark Hankins*
Mark Hankins Ministries

I have known Mark Filkey for nearly thirty years. Mark is a multitalented man of God, preacher, pastor, mentor, musician, worship leader, and author. *Fear Must Not Win* and its timely message come at a critical time for our nation and the world. Faith was designed to conquer fears. You will be encouraged as you read this book.

—*Dick Bernal*
Founder, Jubilee Christian Center, San Jose, CA

There are so many nuggets within this book that speak to my generation. Bishop Filkey's life experiences, discernment, and passion are felt in every word. In a world where it seems as though fear, projected insecurities, and anxiety rule, Bishop Filkey points to a better word, including the triumphant revelation that we are—*by far*—greater than our enemies when we know the One who is standing behind, beside, and before us. We much decide *today* that *Fear Must Not Win*!

—*Doe Jones*
Singer, songwriter, and recording artist

Bishop Mark Filkey is a longtime friend and an uncle to all of my children! For decades, Bishop Filkey has been a blessing not only to our lives but also to the world with his courageous, faith-filled prophetic insights. I believe that *Fear Must Not Win* is a godsend for addressing the troubled times we are living in today. It is truly a must-read book, especially for all those who have never before had the opportunity to benefit from Bishop Filkey's liberating teachings. May your heart and mind be washed clean of all fear as you read through the pages of this book. It is powerful stuff!

—*Dewitt C. Jones III*
Double Grammy-nominated family band forever JONES

Mark Filkey's presentation of the stories and principles in *Fear Must Not Win* is innovative, inspiring, and eye-opening. In an age when the spirit of fear is continually battling to consume our every thought, this book is a great reminder to believers that we have not been given a spirit of fear, but we have been given love—a perfect love that casts out all fear—power, and self-control. For believers, fear must not and cannot win!

—*Pastors Tommy and Brenda Todd*
Transformation Church, Tulsa, OK

Bishop Mark Filkey has declared that *Fear Must Not Win*! Believe me, he has had a lifetime of experience to present a convincing case for attaining fear-free living in this captivating book. His homespun humor, down-to-earth illustrations, and easy-to-grasp, powerful principles make this book an important addition to one's faith library. I love and appreciate Mark Filkey's commitment to establishing a scriptural foundation for confronting and overcoming fear. I hope we can expect more from this unique leader and author.

—*Pastor Denny Duron*
Shreveport Community Church, Shreveport, LA

You never find heroes in smooth times, when everything is right with the world. No, heroes emerge in times of crisis—that's when they go all in! Mark Filkey is such a hero, and he has found the perfect time in our crisis- and anxiety-ridden world to prophesy that *Fear Must Not Win*! As you read this book, the anointing that is on Mark's life for victory and dominion over the spirit of fear will begin to fill your soul. Faith in Christ will arise within you, the peace of God that passes understanding will guard your heart and mind, and you will begin to declare over your own life, "Fear must not win!"

—*Pastor Mel Ayres*
In His Presence Church, Woodland Hills, CA

MARK STEVEN FILKEY

FEAR
MUST NOT WIN

FINDING PEACE, CONFIDENCE, AND COURAGE IN CHALLENGING TIMES

WHITAKER
HOUSE

Scripture quotations marked (NIV) are taken from the *Holy Bible, New International Version*®, NIV®, © 1973, 1978, 1984, 2011 by Biblica, Inc.® Used by permission. All rights reserved worldwide. The "NIV" and "New International Version" are trademarks registered in the United States Patent and Trademark Office by Biblica, Inc.® Scripture quotations marked (ESV) are taken from *The Holy Bible, English Standard Version*, © 2000, 2001, 1995 by Crossway Bibles, a division of Good News Publishers. Used by permission. All rights reserved. Scripture quotations marked (KJV) are taken from the King James Version of the Holy Bible. Scripture quotations marked (KJVER) are taken from the *King James Easy Read Bible*, KJVER®, © 2001, 2007, 2010, 2015 by Whitaker House. Used by permission. All rights reserved. Scripture quotations marked (NKJV) are taken from the *New King James Version*, © 1979, 1980, 1982 by Thomas Nelson, Inc. Used by permission. All rights reserved. Scripture quotations marked (NASB) are taken from the updated *New American Standard Bible*®, © 1960, 1971, 1977, 1995, 2020 by The Lockman Foundation. Used by permission. All rights reserved. (www.Lockman.org). Scripture quotations marked (MSG) are taken from *The Message: The Bible in Contemporary Language* by Eugene H. Peterson, © 1993, 1994, 1995, 1996, 2000, 2001, 2002, 2018. Used by permission of NavPress Publishing Group. All rights reserved. Represented by Tyndale House Publishers, Inc. Scripture quotations marked (NLT) are taken from the *Holy Bible, New Living Translation*, © 1996, 2004, 2015 by Tyndale House Foundation. Used by permission of Tyndale House Publishers, Inc., Carol Stream, Illinois 60188. All rights reserved. Scripture quotations marked (AMP) are taken from *The Amplified® Bible*, © 2015 by The Lockman Foundation, La Habra, CA. Used by permission. (www.Lockman.org). Scripture quotations marked (NIV84) are taken from the *Holy Bible, New International Version*®, NIV®, © 1973, 1978, 1984 by the International Bible Society. Used by permission of Zondervan. All rights reserved. Scripture quotations marked (BST) are from the English translation of The Septuagint by Sir Lancelot Charles Lee Brenton (1851). Scripture quotations marked (YLT) are taken from Young's Literal Translation by Robert Young (1898).

Boldface type in the Scripture quotations indicates the author's emphasis. The forms LORD and GOD (in small capital letters) in Bible quotations represent the Hebrew name for God *Yahweh* (Jehovah), while *Lord* and *God* normally represent the name *Adonai*, in accordance with the Bible version used.

FEAR MUST NOT WIN:
Finding Peace, Confidence, and Courage in Challenging Times

Mark Steven Filkey
www.MarkFilkey.com

ISBN: 978-1-64123-875-5 • eBook ISBN: 978-1-64123-876-2
Printed in the United States of America
© 2022 by Mark Steven Filkey

Whitaker House • 1030 Hunt Valley Circle • New Kensington, PA 15068
www.whitakerhouse.com

LC record available at https://lccn.loc.gov/2022014485
LC ebook record available at https://lccn.loc.gov/2022014486

1 2 3 4 5 6 7 8 9 10 11 🕮 29 28 27 26 25 24 23 22

This book is lovingly dedicated to my wife, Jordana,
and my four sons, Jake, Jordan, Joel, and Jael,
who work beside me, courageously demonstrating
to the world through their daily lives that
Fear Must Not Win.

CONTENTS

ACKNOWLEDGMENTS

I would like to acknowledge all the people in and around my life who have exemplified what authentic faith and calm look like in the face of adversity. I particularly want to recognize my four sons, Jake, Jordan, Joel, and Jael, who fearlessly took the reins while their mother and I were ill and fighting for our lives, especially when the doctors predicted I had less than a 46 percent chance of survival due to acute double pneumonia. Thank you for your relentless spirit of courage and tenacity and for calling family members, friends, and people across the nation to pray on behalf of your mother and me. It is because of your fervent prayers, petitions, and resistance against the powers of darkness that the prayers of God's people prevailed in less than fourteen days, and your mother and I are alive and victorious. To all those who prayed for us without ceasing, thank you!

I also want to acknowledge all of our nation's fearless physicians and other medical professionals; the many courageous men and women in the U.S. military, who serve this country valiantly; our law enforcement officers; and our firefighters and other first responders. Your courage to keep our communities, nation, and world safe epitomizes the true nature of the champion spirit.

In addition, I would like to recognize the brave men and women who are determined to stop human trafficking, illegal drugs, and child pornography. You are the unsung heroes of this era and the defenders of the innocent. Your example is clear proof that there is still hope for our nation and the world.

Finally, I want to acknowledge God-fearing believers everywhere who are no longer willing to settle for the status quo of allowing demonic fear and frustration to be channeled into the innocent hearts and homes of families around the world via the misuse of technology. To all those who have the courage to recognize and refute the unauthorized spirits that are disseminating this fear and frustration, rest assured: your courage is contagious. Together, we can and will make a difference!

There is power in peace,

Mark Steven Filkey

1

"HASH BROWN!": THE POWER OF GOD'S PRESENCE

"You gain strength, courage and confidence by every experience in
which you really stop to look fear in the face.
You are able to say to yourself, 'I have lived through this horror.
I can take the next thing that comes along.' You must do the
thing you think you cannot do."
—*Eleanor Roosevelt*[1]

When I was growing up during in the second half of the twentieth century, I was blessed to experience the freedom to walk or ride my bicycle to
and from just about any place I wanted to go. It was generally an era of
innocence when little boys like my brother and me could go outside and
play all by ourselves without a single care that harm would come to us.
During that era, while there were sobering exceptions, of course, many
children grew up in the same type of free environment.

As a bonus, my father and mother had the presence of mind to move
our family out of the big city—Los Angeles—and into the country. When

1. "Eleanor Roosevelt," Franklin D. Roosevelt Presidential Library and Museum, https://
www.fdrlibrary.org/eleanor-roosevelt.

I was only three years old, we relocated just outside a small farming community in California called Stockton. My father purchased an early-1940s home and had it moved across town, where it rested alongside a quiet, dead-end street nestled between hundreds of unplowed acres and the walnut orchard that sat behind our house.

While my parents felt they had secured a much quieter, safer environment in which to raise my brother and me, it wasn't long before they realized that living out in the middle of nowhere came with its own set of uncertainties and potential dangers, including animals like skunks, raccoons, coyotes, and, at times, wild dogs.

Thankfully, confronting wild animals wasn't something we experienced every day. But my father, having been raised in the city, had somewhere along the way come up with a rapid response for when we did encounter "critters." As crazy as it might seem, this method worked to scare off all unwelcome intruders: he would stand straight up (he was already a tall man), raise his hands, and shout, as loud as he could, "HASH BROWN!"

I particularly remember several occasions when wild animals crept into our front yard—which, incidentally, at that time, was a muddy field—and my father screamed that odd phrase from the deepest place in his lungs, sending those animals scurrying back into the wilderness. I have never been sure why he used the name of a breakfast item to scare off wild animals, but it was certainly effective!

CONFRONTING FEAR

One cold, foggy winter day when I was almost ten, my parents received word that a possible rabies outbreak had occurred in our area. Although I was still young, my father felt he had no choice but to educate me on what to do if I ever found myself face-to-face with a dog or other animal that potentially had been infected with rabies.

I will never forget the feeling that came over me as my dad explained the dangers of being bitten by such a diseased animal. Just hearing the symptoms of rabies—nausea, vomiting, violent movements, uncontrolled anxiety, fear of water, an inability to move parts of one's body, confusion, and even death—would be enough to scare anyone half to death!

Unfortunately, all the little animals around us, including the neighborhood dogs, were prime suspects for carrying and transmitting the disease via bite or saliva.

As I listened with my eyes wide open, trying to absorb all this alarming information, my father added this warning: "Now Marky, listen carefully! If you are ever confronted by an animal that looks infected, don't move forward to approach it, and, whatever you do, don't just turn and run! These animals smell fear. And if you run, they will chase you and bite you! It's not a pleasant thought, and if you trip and fall, they will go for the throat, trying to kill you!"

Taking a deep breath and trying to be brave, I asked, "Then what should I do?" My dad replied, "If possible, quietly back away, nice and easy, until you have an opportunity to get away, and then come home and tell your mother and me." What he said next was something I have never forgotten. His words saved me personally, and I also later told them to my own sons, who are now grown. "Marky, if any of these animals ever gets aggressive and there's nowhere for you to go...." Suddenly, my dad stood up, fully straightened his back, stuck out his chest, raised his hands, and said, "Shout, as loud as you can, 'HASH BROWN!'" When he screamed that phrase, even though I had heard him yell it many times, it scared me all the way to my bones!

Then my father said one last thing that still echoes in my mind as clearly as the day he said it: "Son, remember, you don't have to be afraid of them. Make them afraid of you! Never forget, in their eyes, you are bigger and taller, so, as I taught you, yell much louder than they growl! The truth is, you are much more of a threat to them than they are to you. Do and say what you've seen and heard me do and say a thousand times!" I leaned back, took a breath, and then exhaled as he said, "Do you understand, Son?" Quickly, I responded, "Yes, sir! I got it!"

FIGHT OR FLIGHT?

In my little mind, I continually replayed potential scenarios where I was being either bitten or chased by zombie-looking creatures with red eyes and saliva dripping from their fangs. As you might imagine, I was beyond relieved when I didn't experience any problems in the weeks and months following. I encountered no rabid skunks, squirrels, or coyotes. Thank God!

Then it happened. It was on a Saturday evening more than a year later, just a few weeks after my eleventh birthday. I was walking home from a friend's house through a freshly plowed field when I heard an odd noise behind me. When I turned around to see what I was hearing, I noticed dust off in the distance and the sound of barking dogs, along with an eerie cry. "Oh, no!" I thought. "It can't be!"

I swiped my long hair out of my face, away from my eyes. After struggling to catch a glimpse of what was coming toward me, I finally got a better look at how many wild dogs there were. I worked feverishly to calm myself, trying not to panic.

Quickly, I turned back around, attempting to measure the distance between where the dogs were and the location of my home. Even though I was a relatively short way from the house, my heart began beating rapidly in my chest as my mind tried to decide what to do next. Should I make a run for it? At the time, there were very few neighbors living close to us, so I didn't have the option of running to a nearby house.

Before I knew it, almost as if they were systematically taking turns lunging at me, three wild-looking, four-legged beasts came toward me, tumbling, rolling, and finally skidding to a slow halt. Each of them used its wiry, muscular back legs to force a complete stop. They all landed with their heads down, and they were barking, snarling, and snapping at me as if I were the smaller prey and the battle was about to begin.

It felt like a match to see who was going to back down first.

THEY ALL LANDED WITH THEIR HEADS DOWN, AND THEY WERE BARKING, SNARLING, AND SNAPPING AT ME AS IF I WERE THE SMALLER PREY AND THE BATTLE WAS ABOUT TO BEGIN.

Fight or flight? That was the question. But, in an astonishing moment, my flight for life mechanism kicked in as the scene seemed to shift into slow motion. I cautiously backed away, as my father had taught me to do, but the dogs began to deliberately follow me, as if waiting for me to turn and run. Then, after what seemed like the longest minutes of my life, it was "go time"! Something like a supernatural shadow came over me as I stood straight up, leaned in, took a deep breath, lifted my hands as high and as wide as I could, and let out a shout: "HASH BROWN!"

At that moment, I could hardly believe the animals' startled reactions, but mostly I could barely believe what had just come out of my mouth. As my voice had echoed across the field, it had sounded exactly like my father's voice! Again, I shouted, "HASH BROWN!" I continued to yell in this way, keeping my hands raised over my head, as I advanced toward the animals, driving them further and further backward. Finally, the animals looked at me as if they were facing an army of angels, and, as they turned around, they began to run and yelp as if their tails were on fire! Relieved to finally be able to catch my breath, I leaned forward, placing my hands on my knees, and took a deep breath.

As I worked to regain my composure, I heard a voice right behind me.

MY FATHER'S PRESENCE

Looking backward between my legs, my eyes came into focus, and I saw a tall, courageous figure standing a few feet behind me with that familiar smile on his face. It was my dad! As soon as I saw him, I quickly twisted my body around and ran into his arms. He pulled me close and hugged me, saying, "Good job, Son!" As tears filled my eyes, I asked, "How did you know?" He replied, "It was getting late, and your mother was concerned, so I came looking for you! When I saw you moving toward the dogs, I moved toward them with you! Every time you screamed 'HASH BROWN!' I shouted it behind you!"

I pulled away, smiled, and said, "You mean…?" He answered, "Yep! That wasn't an echo. It was me. I was here shouting and facing those dogs with you the entire time!"

The booming, courageous voice that had shouted and sent those crazy, aggressive animals scurrying back across that field into a distant orchard hadn't been my voice at all. It had been my father's. He had been standing behind me and shouting with me.

I looked back to check on the wild dogs, but they were nowhere to be found. Within seconds, I felt an overwhelming peace come over me. Fear had been swallowed up in victory! Not just by the faith and courage infused into my spirit by my father, but, more important, by the power of my father's voice and presence.

FEAR HAD BEEN SWALLOWED UP IN VICTORY! NOT JUST BY THE FAITH AND COURAGE INFUSED INTO MY SPIRIT BY MY FATHER, BUT, MORE IMPORTANT, BY THE POWER OF MY FATHER'S PRESENCE.

LESSONS LEARNED, FEAR DEFEATED

While this incident happened to my father and me well over fifty years ago, its lessons continue to remind me of just how strong our heavenly Father is. As I reflect on what my dad taught and demonstrated for me while I was growing up, this is the main truth I learned: the presence of God is always there with a big shout against the "giants" of life that seek to cause us fear, dread, anxiety, and panic. In the decades that have followed, I have discovered proven ways to face my fears and defeat those giants in God's strength.

I began this book with the "hash-brown" story because I wanted to emphasize from the start that gaining victory over any type of fear in our lives begins with acknowledging and living in the presence of our heavenly Father. Here are some takeaways from the lessons I have learned, which I will expand on throughout *Fear Must Not Win*:

+ *Your heavenly Father never allows you to face your fears and/or threats alone.* When you are faced with life's challenges—and some of them may well be life-threatening—be assured that your heavenly Father is always with you. Even though you may feel like you are isolated and alone, God is aware when you come under attack, and He runs to the field to meet your enemies with you. You are not alone!

+ *You must learn to confront your fears.* There will be times when you find yourself face-to-face with the kinds of threats and challenges you will not be able to escape or outrun. At those moments, you must turn and boldly face them. Though you may not feel courageous, you *can* stand up against them, knowing that your Father stands with you. Again, whenever it doesn't seem as if God is with you, remember that He is standing behind you, ready to support and protect you in times of trouble.

+ *When a threat feels bigger than you are, the truth is, when you stand up against it, you are always larger than the opposition.* Why? Because greater is He who is in you than anything that comes against you! (See 1 John 4:4.)

+ *You must discover the power of your relationship with God and your position in Him.* When you do this, you can learn how to stand up against both earthly dangers and demonic attacks. Just as the wild dogs ran away when they found themselves face-to-face with the combination of my faith and my earthly father's presence, the devil will put his tail between his legs and run back from where he came when you stand in your faith and in the heavenly Father's presence! *"Submit yourselves therefore to God. Resist the devil, and he will flee from you"* (James 4:7 KJV, KJVER).

+ *Never forget to raise your hands as a sign of victory, even when facing your enemies.* Something shifts in the spiritual realm when you praise God during your battles. Lifted hands represent strength, power, and victorious faith on the field! Nothing frustrates or scares the devil more than a fearless warrior who understands the power of lifted hands and a lifted spirit. In the Bible, we read instances of the Israelites winning battles without firing a single shot but, rather, praising and worshipping God. The enemy is afraid of losing a fight he knows he can't win. When the powers of darkness see you moving forward, full of faith, arms raised in worship, those demonic dogs will run for the hills! They know when they're outnumbered. As you increasingly walk in this exciting lifestyle of faith, you will encounter a powerful truth: your most significant victories are preceded by praise. So, lift your hands and give God all the honor and glory!

+ *Use your voice.* Turn up the volume of your faith by opening your mouth and declaring the truths in God's Word. Words have power, and when you speak the Word, fear flees and walls fall! The Bible says, *"The word of God is...powerful, and sharper than any two-edged sword"* (Hebrews 4:12 KJVER). Along with raising your hands in victory, speak words of faith, prayer, praise, and worship, shouting out to God with the voice of triumph. (See Psalm 47:1.) The faith-infused sound of your voice will send shockwaves up and down the spines of your enemies! Just as those dogs scurried off into the shadows when they heard my voice and the raised voice of my father, your enemies will look for the exit signs when you begin to use your voice in concert with God's Word. Don't wait until the battle is over; shout your praises now!

WHENEVER IT DOESN'T SEEM AS IF GOD IS WITH YOU, REMEMBER THAT HE IS STANDING BEHIND YOU, READY TO SUPPORT AND PROTECT YOU IN TIMES OF TROUBLE.

GOD IS ON YOUR SIDE

Perhaps you're facing what appears to be an impossible test or challenge, and it is provoking feelings of anxiety or dread within you. Or maybe you just need to conquer fear itself. Here is the good news: you can do it! You can be equipped to stand against and defeat every challenging giant that threatens to break you and steal your God-given dreams and destiny.

The psalmist said, *"My enemies would hound me all day, for there are many who fight against me, O Most High. Whenever I am afraid, I will trust in You"* (Psalm 56:2–3 NKJV). Here is a wonderful biblical commentary on this passage:

> Over against God, the majestic One, men are feeble beings. Their rebellion against the counsel of God is ineffective madness. If the poet has God's favour on his side, then he will face these pigmies that behave as though they were giants, who fight against him…, moving on high, i.e., proudly…, in the invincible might of God…. Thus, then, he does not fear; in the day when…he might well be afraid…, he clings trustfully to…his God, so that fear cannot come near him. He has the word of His promise on his side.[2]

Remember, when you are afraid, fully trust in the Lord. He is on your side. Your heavenly Father is greater than your problems. The giants of the world pale in comparison to His splendor. In His presence, problems shrink, and fears dissipate. Ordinary people are formidable and capable of pulverizing walls and obliterating giants if they will believe in the Lord and trust Him. Every situation has a "God solution," and every giant can be conquered.

To have an optimistic attitude based on God's promises is not the same as quoting nice-sounding clichés that ignore reality and tricking ourselves into believing that everything is okay when it's not. Just the opposite: it is a way for us to take the scales of fear and worry off our eyes and see that the One who is for us is greater than all the problems that have come against us. Oral Roberts said, "When you see the invisible, you can do the impossible."[3] Never let worry stop you from seeing what the actual spiritual reality is.

---

2. Keil and Delitzsch, Biblical Commentary on the Old Testament, https://biblehub.com/commentaries/psalms/56-1.htm.
3. Oral Roberts, *When You See the Invisible, You Can Do the Impossible* (Shippensburg, PA: Destiny Image Publishers, 2011).

By God's design, when it comes to dealing with fear, we are created to fight, not to run and hide. Therefore, stand up, push back, and prevail, even in the midst of perplexing and stressful times. Fear often heightens our sense of feeling overwhelmed by our circumstances because we imagine that we are all alone, without any source of help. When your heart seems to fail, let your spiritual eyes "look to the hills from where your help comes." You can rely on the Lord, who made heaven and earth. (See Psalm 121:1–2.) In times of fear, distress, and tragedy, our help comes from God. When we face tests, trials, and tribulations, we can shout, "He comes! He comes to save!"

NEVER LET WORRY STOP YOU FROM SEEING WHAT THE ACTUAL SPIRITUAL REALITY IS.

Just as my father taught me how to stand tall in the face of aggression, you can overcome every fear you can imagine. The heavenly Father wants to teach you how to surmount worry and anxiety in your life and be a conqueror in Christ Jesus. Don't settle for less than God's absolute best for you. *Fear must not win!*

In the following chapters, we will explore common sources of fear, such as the influence of the media in promoting alarm and uncertainty in our lives, childhood trauma, painful memories, and misperceptions. I will walk you through a variety of spiritual techniques centered on prizing God's presence that will strengthen your faith, minimize your panic, counteract fear's power to paralyze, and invite peace into every situation. Through engaging biblical accounts, personal stories, and life lessons, you will learn principles and truths by which you can begin living a fear-free life—the life God always intended for you.

As you read this book, let me encourage you to allow the Holy Spirit to heal you spiritually and emotionally and to inspire you to pursue and fulfill the purpose God has given you. In each chapter, you will discover something powerful about yourself and the God who made you. Just beneath the surface of who you believe you are, there is far more than you have imagined. Let God instill you with the courage to face your fears, rise above your anxieties, push aside dread, and slay your giants!

PART ONE

CONFRONTING OUR FEARS

2

WHEN THE WORLD FEELS LIKE IT'S COMING APART

> "I learned that courage was not the absence of fear, but the triumph over it. The brave man is not he who does not feel afraid, but he who conquers that fear."
> —*Nelson Mandela*[4]

The world around us appears to be unthreading and coming apart at the seams. It often feels like we are experiencing the unfolding of an apocalypse straight out of a made-for-the-silver-screen movie! In fact, in recent times, we have seen scenarios from fictional disaster films become real-life crises in America and around the globe.

FROM FICTION TO REALITY

In the 1970s, a movie called *The Towering Inferno* was released about a massive fire that develops in a brand-new San Francisco skyscraper, the largest building in the world. The blaze, caused by faulty wiring due to the

---

4. Amy McKenna, "15 Nelson Mandela Quotes," Britannica, https://www.britannica.com/list/nelson-mandela-quotes.

irresponsible actions of a subcontractor, occurs during the dedication party for the building. The movie depicts the race to save the lives of the people trapped in the burning structure.

The filmmakers created an imaginary thriller intended to arouse an entertaining, temporary sense of fear in the hearts of audiences and, in the process, generate a box-office hit. After watching the movie, people could meander toward the door of the theater, breathing sighs of relief that the situation wasn't real. Over the years, millions of film fans have watched or rewatched this movie on VHS or DVD or through online streaming services. Each time, they could be comforted by the belief that nothing this horrific could ever happen in real life, at least not in America.

That is, until the morning of September 11, 2001, when a commercial airliner struck the North Tower of the World Trade Center in New York City. People all over America and around the globe turned on their television sets and watched in disbelief as they witnessed the devastating sight of the tower on fire, with scores of people trapped inside. Viewers waited in suspense as TV news crews worked feverishly to report on what had actually occurred, hoping it was a freak accident.

Soon, however, a second plane hit the South Tower, sending plumes of smoke and ash into the New York skyline. As the day unfolded, viewers were stunned to learn that terrorists on a suicide mission had hijacked four commercial airliners. Three of the planes, filled with innocent passengers, flew straight into the Twin Towers and the Pentagon, sending flames and shockwaves worldwide. On the fourth plane, United Flight 93, the crew and passengers discovered what was happening and courageously stormed the terrorists on their plane. As a result, the plane crashed and exploded in a Western Pennsylvania field. Tragically, the lives of the heroic crew members and passengers were lost, but they succeeded in preventing the terrorists from reaching their intended target, likely the U.S. Capitol Building.

The terrorists' mission was clear: *create shock and dread in the hearts of the American people!* Sadly, their plan worked. Our nation would never be the same. The horrific events of that day transformed the way we viewed ourselves, our personal safety, and our national security. And it caused some of our most common patterns of life—including the way we traveled—to be permanently altered.

To give just one example, airport security measures were vastly increased. With only a few exceptions, family members and friends could no longer accompany their traveling loved ones through airports to their gates for departing flights or greet them at their gates when they arrived. Passengers not only had to walk through metal detectors and have their belongings screened, but they also sometimes had to endure body searches by security agents. Airports brought in bomb-sniffing dogs to walk the passenger lines as a means of identifying and thwarting terrorist threats.

TODAY, IT CAN FEEL LIKE WE ARE WITNESSING THE UNFOLDING OF AN APOCALYPSE STRAIGHT OUT OF A MADE-FOR-THE-SILVER-SCREEN MOVIE.

Fast-forward from 2001 to 2011, when theaters across America released a film entitled *Contagion* about a viral outbreak that begins in Hong Kong and becomes a global pandemic causing tens of millions of deaths. In the film, health officials struggle to find the cause and develop a cure. Sound eerily familiar?

Scott Burns, the screenwriter of *Contagion*, wrote in an email to NPR that the filmmakers wanted to tell the story of a "plausible" outbreak—"not a Hollywood exaggeration."

"We were trying to tell a story that was credible within the boundaries of scientific understanding, but also illuminate how our world might respond—that is why the poster of the movie says 'nothing spreads like fear,'" he adds.[5]

Although the film depicted a deadly viral outbreak, it is likely that most of the audiences who saw the movie when it was first released never dreamed a pandemic like that would happen in the real world with such

---

5. Fran Kritz, "Fact-Checking 'Contagion'—In Wake of Coronavirus, the 2011 Movie Is Trending," February 16, 2020, NPR, https://www.npr.org/sections/goatsandsoda/2020/02/16/802704825/fact-checking-contagion-in-wake-of-coronavirus-the-2011-movie-is-trending.

far-reaching consequences. Yet, nine years later, the coronavirus outbreak became a horrific tragedy that has impacted the entire world to the extent that life may never return to pre-pandemic "normal."

Social media sites became filled with posts about the close similarities between what unfolded as a result of the imaginary virus in the film *Contagion* and people's collective experiences with Covid-19. People were saying, "The reality and similarities between the plot of the movie and the pandemic are scary!" A fictional nightmare had become reality.

Not only have we had to face a global pandemic, but we also currently live in an ongoing climate of economic instability, political disorder, social tension, and environmental concerns, including the potential for heightened natural disasters. Our future can look uncertain and frightening. Much of what lies ahead for us appears tenuous, whether we thoughtfully consider our own relationships, finances, and health or warily monitor conflicts between nations, the state of the international economy, and the concerns of global health officials. The world seems to be in a spiritual, cultural, and economic convulsion, making us wonder if we will ever get off this wild roller coaster.

Fear and uncertainty about the future can leave us feeling stressed, anxious, and powerless over the direction of our lives. It can drain us emotionally and trap us in a downward spiral of endless "what ifs" and worst-case scenarios about what tomorrow may bring. If we're not careful, fear will take hold of us as we experience a sense of lost control over critical areas of our lives. Research has shown that *intolerance of uncertainty* can lead to increased levels of angst.[6]

END-TIMES FEARS

In addition to feeling anxious about the fear-inducing circumstances I just described, we sometimes succumb to Satan's attempts to pervert words that God intended to strengthen us into a message that incites alarm in our hearts. Sometimes we forget that the devil is a theologian, in

6. See, for example, Francine Russo, "The Personality Trait 'Intolerance of Uncertainty' Causes Anguish During COVID," Scientific American, February 14, 2022, https://www.scientificamerican.com/article/the-personality-trait-intolerance-of-uncertainty-causes-anguish-during-covid/.

the sense that he knows God's Word. However, instead of obeying it, he tries to use it against us, just as he tried to do with Jesus. (See, for example, Luke 4:1–13.) He understands that we are moving toward the culmination of the ages, and he seeks to attach a sense of fear to the unfolding prophetic events around us in order to rob us of peace and calmness in our souls. If we are not thoroughly immersed in God's presence—and in the truth of His Word—then the powers of darkness can use the very Scriptures God sent to prepare us for the last days to cause us to fear instead. Even the most dedicated Christian is susceptible to falling prey to such oppression.

We are currently witnessing in our world what the Bible describes as *"perilous"* (2 Timothy 3:1, various translations) or *"terrible"* (NIV) times in which there will be a great falling away from the faith. (See verses 2–5; 1 Timothy 4:1.) But even such times are not cause for allowing our fears to control us. Look at what Jesus told His disciples after describing how they would face persecution yet have the constant presence of the Holy Spirit with them: *"These things I have spoken to you, **that in Me you might have peace**. In the world you shall have tribulation: **but be of good cheer**; I have overcome the world"* (John 16:33 KJVER). While there should be no doubt that we are witnessing prophetic times, God's Word reminds us that we are His children and do not need to fear what He sent His Son to save us from and bring us through.

Those who are not yet born again have no such protections and guarantees. Unless they receive God's peace through Christ, their fear of the worsening conditions in our world will continue to grow. The warnings Jesus gave His disciples in Matthew 24 should awaken every unbeliever to the stark reality of the end times so they will turn to God:

> *Take heed that no man deceive you. For many shall come in My name, saying, I am Christ; and shall deceive many. And you shall hear of wars and rumors of wars: **see that you be not troubled**: for all these things must come to pass, but the end is not yet. For nation shall rise against nation, and kingdom against kingdom: and there shall be famines, and pestilences, and earthquakes, in divers places.*
>
> (Matthew 24:4–7 KJVER)

While people have differing opinions about the timing of these events, some believing that they have already occurred, I believe Jesus was clearly warning us about the end times. Perhaps most important, His intention of strengthening and comforting us through His words should be crystal clear! He lovingly tells us, *"See that you be not troubled"* (verse 6). The *Amplified* version reads, *"See that you are not frightened."*

For some people, reading about the last days is a recipe for covering their heads and never coming out of their houses! Yet, while I believe in prophecy, and I sincerely think we are living in the end times, *we cannot and must not allow seeds of fear to be sown into the soil of our hearts*, especially in regard to what God's Word says about the prophetic times in which we are living.

In Luke 21, we are warned of a day when people's hearts would faint because of all that would occur in the latter times: *"People will faint from terror, apprehensive of what is coming on the world, for the heavenly bodies will be shaken"* (Luke 21:26 NIV). Many people today feel they are being tossed around in a spiral of confusion and anxiety. But inside this spiraling disruption, we can still find peace and be redirected to a life in which we are no longer hindered or consumed by fear. We can discover spiritual keys to living in grace and courage at all times and under all circumstances. *"When you are in distress and all these things happen to you, in the latter days **you will return to the Lord your God and listen to His voice**"* (Deuteronomy 4:30 NASB). Shakespeare wrote, "Our doubts are traitors, and makes us lose the good we oft might win by fearing to attempt."[7] In the face of fear, the doubter's door must be slammed shut, never to be opened again, for "God has not given us the spirit of fear; but of power, and of love, and of a sound mind" (2 Timothy 1:7 KJVER).

WE CAN DISCOVER SPIRITUAL KEYS TO LIVING IN GRACE AND COURAGE AT ALL TIMES AND UNDER ALL CIRCUMSTANCES.

---

7. J. W. Lever, ed., *Measure for Measure*, reprint ed. (London: Arden Shakespeare, 2004; North Yorkshire: Methuen & Company Ltd, 1965), 1.4.78–79. References are to act, scene, and lines.

"THEY WILL WALK AND NOT FAINT"

God has assured us that He will never leave or forsake us. (See, for example, Deuteronomy 31:6; Hebrews 13:5.) And Jesus said, *"I am with you always, even to the end of the world"* (Matthew 28:20 KJVER). As you will see throughout this book, living in fear—no matter what the cause of that fear—is not what God intended for His children. Ever.

Isaiah 40 has a wonderful answer for apprehension, discouragement, and fear:

> [The Lord] *gives power to the faint; and to them that have no might He increases strength. Even the youths shall faint and be weary, and the young men shall utterly fall: but they that wait upon the LORD shall renew their strength; they shall mount up with wings as eagles; they shall run, and not be weary; and they shall walk, and not faint.*
>
> (Isaiah 40:29–31 KJVER)

In the late 1990s, my wife, Jordana, and I, along with our four sons, had the privilege of visiting our good friends Pastors Phil and Faye Marocco, who were pastoring two churches on Kauai, the "Garden Island" of Hawaii. One of their congregations met in a former shopping mall on the property of a large, luxurious hotel on the beach. The other congregation was blessed to gather in a small chapel located on a beautiful mountainside, and I was scheduled to speak at that location on our first Sunday there. When the service concluded that Sunday, the Maroccos asked us if we would be interested in seeing something we had never seen before. All our boys answered with a resounding, "Yes!"

We followed the Maroccos' car to the destination, and, within minutes, we pulled into a small, red dirt parking lot with an old weathered sign that read:

Kauai Animal Shelter

Everyone Welcome!

As we got out of our car, the boys began to shout, "It's a zoo!"

"Well, not exactly," Phil replied, "but close! It's actually an animal shelter where they care for abandoned animals."

Phil, the boys, and I passed through the first gate and soon came to an old, hand-painted sign with an arrow on it that read, "Goats This Way." At a good pace, we followed Phil down a small path, encountering many different kinds of animals—rabbits, pot-bellied pigs, large reptiles, and some strange-looking animals we had never seen before. Then Phil slowed down and pointed to a fenced-off section of the shelter with a sign that read:

Quiet Please!

Don't Startle the Goats!

We walked through a small wooden gate that led to the goat area, and the boys started to get excited, so they picked up their pace. Phil advised, "Wait a minute, guys! I want to show you the reason I brought you up here."

Jokingly, I asked, "Phil, you brought us all this way to see some Hawaiian goats?" Everyone laughed, and then Phil paused before saying, "Yes, but these aren't your normal, everyday, run-of-the-mill goats! They have a crazy secret!"

He continued, "The only thing about these little guys that makes them Hawaiian is that they were left here on the island by their former owners. But that's not what makes these goats so unique! What makes these goats so—"

Before he could finish his sentence, the owner of the shelter walked up to greet us. "Pastor Phil," he said, "who do you have here with you?"

"These are my good friends from California. They're here on the island to speak to our church on the mountain. Today, Pastor Mark spoke on the subject of faith versus fear!" He smiled at the owner in a knowing way and continued, "I wanted to show Mark the goats!"

"Oh, okay," the owner said, "I get it! Well, any friends of Phil and Faye are friends of ours!" When Phil finished introducing us, the owner turned around, grabbed a large plastic bag, reached into it, and produced two large handfuls of freshly cut apples and some carrots. "Here are some goodies so you can feed these guys. They especially love the carrots!"

Thinking Phil might be playing a joke on us, I pressed him a little further, asking, "So what do these special goats do, exactly, Pastor Phil? Do they roll over like dogs? Jump? Fly?"

With a big smile on his face, he lifted up a couple of the carrots, leaned forward, and said, "Just watch." He held the carrots in plain sight where the goats could see them. Three of the larger, more plump-looking animals, which had been lying down, jumped to their hooves and came trotting across the yard toward us.

Suddenly, Phil shouted, "BOO, GOATS!" In a flash, all three goats suddenly twirled, stiffened up like a board, and rolled over onto the red dirt!

Shocked, we all asked, "What just happened? Are they okay?"

"They're absolutely fine!" Phil replied. Seconds later, all three goats popped right back up as if nothing had happened and started making their way toward us again. When they reached the halfway point, Phil again shouted at them, calling, "HEY, GOATS!"

This time, every goat within hearing distance immediately stiffened up and twirled over onto the red dirt—some with their legs sticking out sideways and others with their legs sticking straight up in the air, as if they were paralyzed.

I looked at Phil incredulously and asked, "What in the world?" Seconds later, every goat in the yard was back up on its hooves and moving toward us. They all finally arrived at the place where Phil stood, and they feasted on the carrots and apples. Phil handed the bag of food to the boys and motioned for me to follow him to a shade tree to get out of the heat. Then he began to explain, telling me that, in the morning service, as I had read the passage from Isaiah that says, "They shall run, and not grow weary; they shall walk, and not faint," he had suddenly thought of these goats. He asked me, "Did you see their reaction when I scared them? Fear or shock paralyzes them. When they are startled, they panic, freeze up, and fall down. They are out like a light. They can't think, and, most of all, they can't move!"

He had my full attention. "Do all goats do this?" I asked.

"No, these animals are called 'fainting goats' for a reason. Interestingly, they are born with this characteristic. It's passed down to them. It's in their DNA."

Finally, the owner walked over to us and jokingly asked, "Pastor Phil, are you through scaring my goats?" and we all laughed.

After that, we continued to have a wonderful time visiting and ministering with Pastors Phil and Faye. It was a memorable trip.

Over the years, I've told this story at a number of conferences. The audience always erupts into laughter, and I enjoy sharing this incident. Then I make a connection between those goats and us humans! While we may not like being compared to fainting goats, we can actually learn something important from them.

The goats' behavior is an inherited reaction to shock. They are born with this propensity to become paralyzed and to faint when they are startled or scared. It's not something they can control. We, too, have an ingrained tendency to "faint" when we experience something unexpected, disquieting—or, worse, unimaginable. Sadly, this "fainting condition" is in our human DNA. When we are exposed to a difficult or traumatic experience, it can paralyze us, cutting us off from other people and hindering us from pursuing God's purposes for us.

To be clear, the issue isn't the difficult or traumatic experience itself. It is in the way we react or deal with the experience. It is in our fallen nature to "fall down" in fear or despair at times when we are challenged or attacked, or when we experience pain and suffering. The good news is that Jesus paid the price to free us from this generational curse. He shed His blood to remove all those natural frailties that cause us to be paralyzed in troubling times. This means that we are no longer "goats." We are the sheep of God's pasture, and He is our Good Shepherd. (See, for example, Psalm 100:3.)

Satan is in the business of both initiating and using shocking events to take us out of the equation. He knows very well who we are in Christ and how we are able to thwart his kingdom of darkness when we operate in God's strength and not our own. In Isaiah 40, the prophet Isaiah predicted a day when a courageous generation would arise that would not faint but instead walk steadily and run swiftly in God's strength!

The masses around us are freezing up and fainting for fear because of all that is happening in the world today. But because God is with us, even in the most extreme circumstances, we no longer have to be afraid. When we find ourselves walking through what feels like the valley of the shadow of death, we do not have to fear evil. (See Psalm 23:4 KJV, KJVER, NKJV.) God gives us the power of His presence and Spirit, who leads, guides, and comforts us.

It is time to turn the tables by paralyzing the powers of darkness! When we acknowledge the Lord instead of freezing up and fainting, hell gets nervous. When we pray, worship, and praise God in startling times, demons freeze in their tracks and fall to the ground or run for the exit signs.

Through His victory on the cross, Jesus has given us the ability to stand and not faint in the day of adversity. We have power through Christ to thrive in times of trouble. No more falling prey to the enemy's shock treatment. No more freezing up. No more fainting. We will not allow anything or anyone to paralyze us. Instead, we will rise to up to reclaim all the territory Satan has stolen from our lives and the lives of others.

BECAUSE GOD IS WITH US, EVEN IN THE MOST EXTREME CIRCUMSTANCES, WE NO LONGER HAVE TO BE AFRAID.

COURAGEOUS JOURNEY—OR DEAD END?

As the saying goes, "In the end, it's not the years in your life that count. It's the life in your years."[8] When we face personal, medical, social, economic, and political challenges, our lives can be either a courageous journey

---

8. The authorship of this quote is not fully known. It has been tentatively attributed to Dr. Edward J. Stieglitz. See https://quoteinvestigator.com/2012/07/14/life-years-count/.

filled with strength, joy, and love or a meaningless dead end where fear dwells. We are all aware of many things that can provoke fear in us and in others. But we need to learn what *stimulates faith* in us—the faith of God Himself. Remember, "*God has not given us the spirit of fear; but of power, and of love, and of a sound mind*" (2 Timothy 1:7 KJVER).

The author of Psalm 91 wrote, "*Do not be afraid of the terrors of the night, nor the arrow that flies in the day. Do not dread the disease that stalks in darkness, nor the disaster that strikes at midday*" (Psalm 91:5–6 NLT). How can we possibly live free of fear in the midst of night terrors, flying arrows, disease, and disaster? The answer comes at the beginning of the psalm:

> *Those who live in the shelter of the Most High will find rest in the shadow of the Almighty.* This I declare about the Lord: He alone is my refuge, my place of safety; he is my God, and I trust him. For he will rescue you from every trap and protect you from deadly disease. He will cover you with his feathers. He will shelter you with his wings. His faithful promises are your armor and protection. (Psalm 91:1–4 NLT)

Amid the challenges of our day, God is building an army of courageous warriors who refuse to run or hide, men and women who find their strength and refuge in their King. These fearless warriors understand their heavenly assignments, which include canceling fear's mission to debilitate us. In the strength of God's mighty power, we can annul the assignment of the demonic spirit of fear, not only to elude its dangers in the physical world but also to unravel the havoc the devil attempts to wreak in our hearts and in the hearts of our children.

Satan might believe he has succeeded in his quest to instill fear in the lives of those who have not yet received Christ or been filled with His Spirit, but the enemy will not succeed in the lives of born-again believers who dare to rise to the occasion in the strength of the Lord. We would rather die standing straight up in the fiery furnace of affliction than give up and bow down in the midst of those flames. For those of us who are filled with the Spirit of almighty God, when anxiety and dread encroach upon us, remaining in fear is not an option. As we face fear's challenge, we might bend, but we will not be broken!

3

THREE KINDS OF FEAR

"How little can be done under the spirit of fear."
—*Florence Nightingale*[9]

Throughout this book, as we explore the various sources of fear and how to live free of anxiety and dread, we need to understand that not all fear is the same. There is a clear distinction between the three kinds of fear we can experience: (1) godly, natural fear; (2) ungodly, irrational fear; and (3) demonically induced fear.

First, a natural type of fear has been hardwired into us by our Creator to help keep us safe from spiritual, physical, and emotional danger. Second, ungodly fear was unleashed in the lives of all human beings through the fall; this fear is often irrational. It is not based on the spiritual reality of God and His Word but on human circumstances or imagined threats. Such ungodly fear endangers our peace or, worse, keeps us from fulfilling our God-given purposes and destinies. Third, demonic powers, seeking to

---

9. "Florence Nightingale Quote," LibQuotes, https://libquotes.com/florence-nightingale/quote/lbg0w9r.

cause disruption and destruction, attempt to propagate fear in us and in the world around us.

GODLY, NATURAL FEAR

The central aspect of godly fear is "the fear of the Lord," which refers to a deep reverence and respect for God, His power, and His righteousness. In Proverbs 14:27, Solomon declared, *"The fear of the LORD is a fountain of life, by which one may avoid the snares of death"* (NASB). Having a healthy fear of the Lord is *"a fountain of life"* because it keeps us within God's will and ways. This type of fear is characterized by an attentive awe and worship of the Lord, along with a strong, holy desire to please Him. It is reflected in the way we live, which includes rejecting sin and not placing our ultimate confidence in ourselves but in the Lord. Those who fear the Lord are spiritually sensitive to Him and continually grow in their ability to tune in to His ongoing guidance for their lives.

God's gift of natural fear also includes an ability to sense, feel, and recognize elements and situations in the material world that would place us in harm's way. Natural fear is an emotion or instinct that alerts us to potential imminent harm so that we will proceed with caution. This type of fear helps to preserve us throughout our lives, especially as we grow from childhood to adulthood, learning about the potential physical dangers around us. When you experience perceived danger, your body produces adrenaline to enable you to react and move far more quickly than usual. The purpose of godly fear is to motivate us to remain in, or get back to, a place of safety.

Most people, through this natural ability, perceive real threats from the material world (although the level and extent of the perceived dangers will vary depending on the individual). For instance, when certain physical elements come near you—a poisonous snake suddenly crosses your path, you notice a shark moving toward you while you are swimming in the ocean, you see a spinning tornado coming in your direction—your brain recognizes it as a danger. As a result, your body automatically reacts with a fight, flight, or freeze response in order to preserve your life.

While such responses are physiological, they are triggered by psychological fear. Often, the fear has also been conditioned, which means you have associated the situation or thing with negative consequences. A psychological response to danger is initiated when you're first exposed to a particular threat or to knowledge about a potential danger; this response is then reinforced over time as the experience or information is repeated. An excellent term for this godly aspect of fear might be an "alarm," a divinely provided mental or emotional bell that goes off, warning you of the real possibility of peril. Your human sensitivity to threat tells you that you must approach with caution—or not approach at all!

We may face physical dangers not only from natural elements but also from various attacks by other human beings. At those times, we need to be able to perceive the situations as God does. This was the case with an incident in the life of the prophet Elisha recorded in 2 Kings 6. One morning, when Elisha's servant got up early and went outside, he was stunned to see the Aramean army surrounding the city where they lived. This army was following orders from the king of Aram to capture Elijah. The servant was terrified because he thought the attack would mean the end for them. In great fear, he rushed back inside to tell Elisha the news.

But Elisha and his servant had two very different responses to this frightening scenario. Elisha was relatively calm because he looked at the situation with a different set of eyes. What you see determines how you act. Elisha prayed that God would open the servant's eyes so that he would see that there were greater forces acting on their behalf than there were enemies acting against them. Though the enemies were all the servant could see, the reality was that God had filled the mountain with *"horses and chariots of fire"* (2 Kings 6:17, various translations), an army from God, sent as divine protection. Like the prophet of old, when we are surrounded by opposition that is apparently greater than we are, we can know that God's presence and power are superior to the enemies that have come against us.

WHAT YOU SEE DETERMINES HOW YOU ACT.

Another applicable term for a godly type of fear might be "concern." This innate, God kind of concern could even be summed up as "wisdom." Wisdom includes the ability to identify, discern, and avoid whatever threatens God's gift of health, well-being, and purpose for us.

The apostle Peter taught us to be *vigilant*, not fearful: *"Be self-controlled and alert. Your enemy the devil prowls around like a roaring lion looking for someone to devour"* (1 Peter 5:8 NIV84). As we reverence the Lord and seek His will for our lives, and as we yield to the leading of His Spirit, we will develop a sensitivity to spiritual threats and learn to counteract them with power, love, and a sound mind.

UNGODLY, IRRATIONAL FEAR

The second category of fear is "ungodly, irrational fear." Most of us have a few fears that can loosely be described as irrational, such as a fear of flying on an airplane or a dread of visiting the dentist. However, some people's inordinate fears can interfere with their daily lives and cause them exceptional stress. An unnatural fear might be described as an excessive or unmerited sense of terror. Psychologists call such an intense fear a "phobia." A phobia is generally characterized by a persistent and extreme anxiety of a particular object or situation. Here are some examples: a fear of being out in public, a fear of being in a confined space, a fear of thunder and lightning, a fear of animals, and a fear of germs. There are many other types of phobias.

People who struggle with phobias often experience stress and anxiety despite being given evidence that their sense of feeling threatened is unfounded. For a number of people, their fear may be rooted in past negative experiences that they are unable to move on from. Make no mistake about it: phobias may have a genuine basis. However, whether they are fully imagined or based on real events, they can demoralize people's lives until they are addressed. Unauthorized or ungodly fear will weaken you by eating away at all that God has designed you to be and to achieve in your life.

Ungodly fear elicits intense anxiety because it is tethered to thoughts that do not come from the knowledge and wisdom of the Lord. This kind of fear always—and I do mean *always*—causes its victims to feel power-less, vulnerable, and unable to control what is occurring in and/or around them. In contrast, godly fear is accompanied by a sense of peace, wisdom, comfort, and control.

First John 4:18 provides great counsel for times when we experience ungodly fear: "*There is no fear in love; but perfect love casts out fear: because fear has torment. He that fears is not made perfect in love*" (KJVER). And, in Romans 8:15, the apostle Paul contributed the following words of encour-agement: "*For you have not received the spirit of bondage again to fear; but you have received the Spirit of adoption, whereby we cry, Abba, Father*" (KJVER).

We can learn to rest in the knowledge of our heavenly Father's perfect love and care for us. As we cultivate godly fear, we can know that God will give us the wisdom to avoid anything that might endanger us. We can hold on to His promises that He will never leave us or forsake us (see, for exam-ple, Deuteronomy 31:6, 8; Hebrews 13:5) and will preserve us through His Spirit of peace and power (see, for example, 1 Thessalonians 5:23).

DEMONICALLY INDUCED FEAR

King Solomon, perhaps the wisest ruler ever to live, wrote, "*I returned, and saw under the sun, that the race is not to the swift, nor the battle to the strong, neither yet bread to the wise, nor yet riches to men of understanding, nor yet favor to men of skill; but time and chance happens to them all*" (Ecclesiastes 9:11 KJVER). In plain, everyday language, this verse might be interpreted as follows: "No one is exempt from life's challenges, which include unex-pected circumstances, turns of events, and attacks. In a race, the fastest runner does not always win the prize, because something or someone may block them, causing them to fall, or they may become lame and have to slow down or stop, causing them to lose the contest."

In other words, sometimes, life's troubles are not because "the devil did it"; instead, they are among the inevitable difficulties that occur in a fallen world. However, at other times, our troubles are caused by the devil essentially throwing spears at us or creating roadblocks in our way. "*For we do not wrestle against flesh and blood, but against the rulers, against the authorities, against the cosmic powers over this present darkness, against the spiritual forces of evil in the heavenly places"* (Ephesians 6:12 ESV).

The devil is a shrewd, time-tested strategist. He often pursues people early in their lives when they are more vulnerable to fear, feeding on that susceptibility. For the less vulnerable, he patiently waits for a ripe opportunity to attack. Satan and his minions seek to influence us both covertly and overtly for the purpose of driving us to accept fear and turmoil in our lives.

We could say that our souls—unless they have God's peace—are the devil's workshop. Covertly, the enemy attempts to spread seeds of doubt in our minds and feelings of fear in our emotions to create bondage, weaken our wills, uproot our lives, and disrupt our futures. His mission is to strike, cripple, and paralyze.

Using a figure of speech for Satan that the Pharisees apparently didn't understand, Jesus spoke of the enemy's destructive ways in this manner: *"The thief comes only to steal and kill and destroy…"* (John 10:10 NASB). Minister and Greek scholar Rick Renner wrote a creative interpretation of the enemy's schemes based on this first portion of John 10:10:

> The goal of this thief is to totally waste and devastate your life. If nothing stops him, he'll leave you insolvent, flat broke, and cleaned out in every area of your life. You'll end up feeling as if you are finished and out of business! Make no mistake—the enemy's ultimate aim is to obliterate you….[10]

We must not allow Satan or any of his demonic minions to steal our lives or our children's lives. Remember that Jesus concluded His statement in John 10:10 by saying that He Himself had come *"so that [we] would have life, and have it abundantly"* (John 10:10 NASB). And the apostle John assured us: *"Greater is He who is in you than he who is in the world"* (1 John 4:4 NASB).

While it is true that no one is exempt from Satan's attacks, this does not mean that God legally sanctions these assaults. He does not! They are illegal and unauthorized. Because you are a child of God, the enemy has no legal right to touch you. You are not his property! Everything about you

---

10. Rick Renner, "The Devil Has a Plan for Your Life!" https://renner.org/article/the-devil-has-a-plan-for-your-life/.

belongs to God, including your mind, will, and emotions. Our heavenly Father is in the business of repairing the damage the enemy has inflicted on you by renewing your mind, strengthening your will, and healing your emotions.

Through the redemption of His Son and the power of His Spirit, God will restore your life to what He originally designed it to be. Our heavenly Father does not create anything without intention, and He does not make anything irrelevant or inferior. When you understand that God created you thoughtfully and intentionally—that your life is *on purpose* and *for a purpose*—then, no matter what the circumstances look like, your fear will begin to dissipate.

And there is more good news: you have also been given spiritual weapons that will enable you to deflect, thwart, and overthrow the devil's destructive plans. (See, for example, Ephesians 6:10–18.) Through Jesus, you can have victory over the enemy's schemes. The devil's program is designed to paralyze you in fear, but God's plan is to preserve you and to empower you in love. The Lord stretches His hand toward you to comfort you and give you the ability to recognize, avoid, and terminate all demonic threats to your well-being.

WHEN YOU UNDERSTAND THAT GOD CREATED YOU ON PURPOSE AND FOR A PURPOSE, *THEN, NO MATTER WHAT THE CIRCUMSTANCES LOOK LIKE, YOUR FEAR WILL BEGIN TO DISSIPATE.*

Wherever Satan seeks to initiate and perpetuate terror, God gives us the power to pull down demonic strongholds and cast down ungodly thoughts. (See 2 Corinthians 10:4–5.) We are anointed to stand against satanic opposition and boldly declare God's promises, which are *"Yes"* and *"Amen"*! (See 2 Corinthians 1:20, various translations.)

The pressure-tested spiritual warrior by the name of the apostle Paul wrote these words to the Corinthian church, reminding those early believers (and us) of their hidden "treasure in earthen vessels"—a treasure from God that is more potent than we may have imagined:

> But we have this treasure in earthen vessels, that the excellency of the power may be of God, and not of us. We are troubled on every side, yet not distressed; we are perplexed, but not in despair; persecuted, but not forsaken; cast down, but not destroyed; always bearing about in the body the dying of the Lord Jesus, that the life also of Jesus might be made manifest in our body.   (2 Corinthians 4:7–10 KJV)

WHERE PEACE IS FOUND

In this book, as we continue to look at truths and principles for defeating fear, you will come to see more clearly how God is an empowering presence in your life, enabling you to overcome all ungodly and demonically induced fears. As I described in chapter 1, while fear is a real emotion, we can survive and triumph in challenging times by learning to live in the presence of God, where peace is found and where our courage can be supernaturally sustained by His Spirit through faith.

4

FEAR SELLS!

"The presence of fear does not mean you have no faith. Fear visits everyone. But make your fear a visitor and not a resident."
—*Max Lucado*[11]

Suppose an enemy agent wanted to infiltrate a nation and attack its people's peace of mind. What would be the best method of disturbing the citizens' mental and emotional peace—or, even better, removing it altogether? One significant way would be to influence the environment around them so that it would perpetuate feelings of insecurity and anxiety.

While, in years past, creating such a widespread environment of fear might have seemed impossible, it is now essentially achievable. Our world's modern technological capabilities, and the way they are being abused, greatly contribute to an atmosphere of ongoing alarm in our society and in other nations around the world. And the powers of darkness are using this situation to their full advantage.

There is an enlightening article in *Quartz* magazine that identifies how people's fear and outrage are being marketed for profit through technology. Here is an excerpt from that article:

---

11. "Max Lucado Quotes," AZ Quotes, https://www.azquotes.com/quote/568754.

Every time you open your phone or your computer, your brain is walking onto a battleground. The aggressors are the architects of your digital world, and their weapons are the apps, news feeds, and notifications in your field of view every time you look at a screen.

They are all attempting to capture your most scarce resource—your attention—and take it hostage for money. Your captive attention is worth billions to them in advertising and subscription revenue.[12]

When I first read this article, I wondered how many readers would recognize just how spiritually parabolic those words are. While the author artfully describes what is happening to people due to various influences from the digital world, we need to understand just how close his words are to what is occurring in the spiritual realm that digital technology helps to facilitate. As you are about to discover, there's far more going on around us than what our eyes see and our ears hear.

FEAR 24/7

Advances in technology and the accessibility of a continual stream of news and entertainment programs have their advantages, and we've come to take their presence for granted. However, we don't always consider their potential negative effects on us. It's often hard to remember that such conveniences weren't always available. When I was young, our family's television set could receive only three channels. TV stations began their broadcast days about six in the morning and signed off between eleven and twelve at night. At that time, a television set received its signal through an antenna located at the back of the set or, at best, on the rooftop of a home or business. Even the strongest antennas might have helped to catch the signal of only one additional channel—that is, if they were close enough to a tower that was broadcasting that signal.

At the end of each broadcast day, stations would play "The Star-Spangled Banner" as they showed film footage of military jets flying and American flags waving. There would also be a voice-over, with an announcer

---

12. Tobias Rose-Stockwell, "This Is How Your Fear and Outrage Are Being Sold for Profit," *Quartz*, July 28, 2017, https://qz.com/1039910/how-facebooks-news-feed-algorithm-sells-our-fear-and-outrage-for-profit/.

saying something like, "This concludes our broadcast day. Thank you for watching. We will resume our broadcast tomorrow morning at six a.m. Until then, good night, God bless you, and God bless America." The patriotic film footage would be replaced by color bars until, finally, there would be no image on the screen at all except for static—fuzzy-looking, salt-and-pepper nothingness.

Consequently, by eleven or twelve at night, people would turn off their television sets, go to bed, and rest their minds until the following morning. Many families didn't watch their TV sets after nine or ten o'clock anyway because programs were limited, including the evening news.

Those days gone by were certainly not without their challenges. However, in many ways, they were less stressful because people were not continually bombarded by news stories and other programming. While, each day, breaking news—communicated via newspapers, radio, and television—captured the attention of millions of people, and there were certain ongoing stories that people followed for a few days or even months at a time, the media was not the fear-mongering machine it has become today. News reports were generally given only once or twice a day as events unfolded. As a result, people had time to process what they had learned before being given additional information.

Today, if you're looking for something to worry about, you don't have to go far. Alarming, attention-grabbing sound bites and imagery are readily accessible twenty-four hours a day, seven days a week. On certain networks and on the Internet, stories are presented over and over again, covering every minutia of an unfolding event. In addition, even as recent as a couple of decades ago, news reports were usually divided into local, national, and international coverage. Those lines have been erased. It seems as if any local story can become a national story, whether or not it has nationwide implications, if it might grab the attention of audiences.

Moreover, today's news networks—whether they communicate through broadcast television, cable, online streaming and websites, or other avenues—seem to earn their money not only by reporting the news but also by *creating* it. Worse yet, some networks have begun to weaponize the news for profit and, in some cases, for personal agendas.

Whereas networks once reported the news as it unfolded, they now often work around the clock to generate, shape, and spin the news into a particular product that sells—and that product is often *fear*. Advertising sponsors want the attention of the masses so badly that they are willing to pay millions of dollars to get it. Because the networks need the sponsors' advertising revenue, they can feel pressured to do whatever it takes to capture and keep the attention of their audiences, even if it includes producing an atmosphere of anxiety and frustration to draw people in.

In times past, many advertisers sought to place their commercials among family entertainment programs, but now they tend to pay vast sums of money to position their commercials on news programs. Massive corporations and marketing companies pay billions of dollars to have their ads run among the most fear- and frustration-fueled programming. The reason is painfully obvious: these companies have learned the nasty secret that fear, frustration, controversy, and divisiveness sell. It's the fear factor, the jolt of presenting a surprising or disturbing turn of events. Fear is very effective bait, and you and I are the "fish."

The more the news programs can create such negative bait, the larger the number of viewers they can capture, and the greater their influence and revenue will be, because a rise in viewership converts into increased advertising dollars. Advertisers are promoting media convulsions to sell their products. All of this translates into one thing: fear and frustration sell. And it is adversely affecting us!

WHEREAS NETWORKS ONCE REPORTED THE NEWS AS IT UNFOLDED, THEY NOW OFTEN WORK AROUND THE CLOCK TO GENERATE, SHAPE, AND SPIN THE NEWS INTO A PARTICULAR PRODUCT THAT SELLS— AND THAT PRODUCT IS OFTEN FEAR.

INFORMATION SUPERHIGHWAYS

To demonstrate just how powerful news corporations can be, in 2009, even at the tail end of the recession of that time, "Fox saw profits grow

19% to $535 million on revenue growth of 14% to $1.21 billion, according to data from SNL Kagan."[13] And that was long before news networks covered the heated election cycles of 2016 and 2020, as well as recent escalated racial divides, social unrest, rioting and looting, police brutality, mass shootings, unstable foreign relations, and a worldwide pandemic.

As indicated previously, news reporting is no longer relegated to cable, satellite, or the good old airwaves but also includes the vast arena of the Internet. In 2021, Google News, owned by Alphabet, Inc., broke two hundred billion dollars in revenue for the first time. "For full-year 2021, the company saw a 41 percent year-over-year jump in revenue to $257 billion."[14] Facebook brought in almost $118 billion in revenues in 2021, with a net profit of $39.3 billion.[15] Today, "2.76 billion people log in daily to one of Facebook's family-owned services, which include WhatsApp, Messenger, and Instagram." Monthly users of Facebook and its platforms reach about 3.5 billion people.[16] In case you read that last statistic rather quickly, that number incorporates a large portion of the planet's entire population, which is approaching 8 billion.

Facebook and Google have become so powerful that many people refer to them as a "duopoly," a term coined from the word *monopoly*. A monopoly refers to "the exclusive possession or control of the supply of or trade in a commodity or service."[17] A duopoly is defined as "a situation in which two suppliers dominate the market for a commodity or service."[18] The key words here are *control* and *dominate*. And gaining and retaining advertisers is a key component of success.

13. "The State of the News Media," Pew Project for Excellence in Journalism, https://assets.pewresearch.org/files/journalism/State-of-the-News-Media-Report-2010-FINAL.pdf.
14. Kim Lyons, "Google Parent Company Alphabet Broke $200 Billion in Annual Revenue for the First Time," February 1, 2022, https://www.theverge.com/2022/2/1/22912196/google-alphabet-200-billion-annual-revenue-youtube-pixel-search.
15. Mansoor Iqbal, "Facebook Revenue and Use Statistics (2022)," Business of Apps, June 8, 2022, https://www.businessofapps.com/data/facebook-statistics/.
16. Brian Dean, "Facebook Demographic Statistics: How Many People Use Facebook in 2022?" January 5, 2022, https://backlinko.com/facebook-users, accessed June 12, 2022.
17. *Lexico*, s.v., "monopoly," https://www.lexico.com/en/definition/monopoly.
18. *Lexico*, s.v., "duopoly," https://www.lexico.com/en/definition/duopoly.

The Social Media Advertising market is the second biggest market within Digital Advertising. The worldwide revenue of US$153.7 billion in 2021 is expected to grow to US$252.6 billion in 2026.[19]

While a certain amount of what is presented on social media is positive, much of it is negative. Scores of people are daily being bombarded by an overwhelming number of negative images, sound bites, and gossip. They soak up other users' emotionally charged opinions and information (including misinformation) about the world around them. For those who intentionally and systematically disseminate negative information, it often means dollar signs and vast dividends, including a powerful influence over the masses.

Sadly, because of the spiritually weak condition of the current generation, negativity sells, alarm is profitable, and shock rules. People are drawn to negative stories and reports. Again, media outlets are involved in an ongoing race to gain more viewers so they can increase their influence, and corporations can multiply their revenue through strategically placed advertisements. It's a vicious cycle! Add to the mix social media application technology, which facilities an unending flow of all of the above content via so-called smart devices, and, presto, you have a dark and destructive situation.

A SPIRITUAL SUPERHIGHWAY

Most people focus on the bright side of the digital world. However, it is increasingly observable that social media presents enormous risks for individuals, communities, companies, and society as a whole. Examples of social media's dark side include cyberbullying, addictive use, trolling, pornography, online witch hunts, fake news, and privacy abuse.

The underbelly of this dark side is the spiritual superhighway through which demonic powers traverse without restraint. While many believers have never made the connection, this is Satan's new path of disseminating fear and impregnating people with worry. Job 1:7 gives us an illustration of Satan's determination to gain access to people through any source and

19. "Digital Advertising Report 2021—Social Media Advertising," Statista, https://www. statista.com/study/36294/digital-advertising-report-social-media-advertising/, accessed June 12, 2022.

means he can: "*The* LORD *said to Satan, 'Where have you come from?' Satan answered the* LORD*, 'From roaming throughout the earth, going back and forth on it'*" (Job 1:7 NIV). In the *New Living Translation*, this verse reads, "'*Where have you come from?' the* LORD *asked Satan. Satan answered the* LORD*, 'I have been patrolling the earth, watching everything that's going on.'*"

When we closely consider the words "*patrolling the earth,*" it is not difficult to imagine how Satan's traversing the globe would lead him to the digital world as a means of gaining continual access to people's ear gates and eye gates. Our ear gates and eye gates receive not only neutral sound bites and information, but also deceptive talking points and propaganda spewed forth from the powers of darkness to influence gatekeepers.

Such a scenario may or may not surprise you. Either way, be assured that evil spiritual powers are, through human agents, using the tools of technology to gain access to multitudes of souls. There is a rudimentary reason for Satan to do this: what better way to alienate people from God and destroy them than to use the direct access of digital avenues such as smart devices, computers, and televisions to disseminate fear? The final result is the seduction of the minds, wills, and emotions of men, women, boys, and girls everywhere. Their unguarded souls are vulnerable to ungodly spirits that initiate and perpetuate confusion, distress, and horror.

Today, millions of people are—for a variety of reasons—anxious and restless. Many don't sleep well at night. In some instances, they can't function without anti-anxiety or anti-depression medications. Doctors are prescribing drugs to help patients cope with all the fear that is infecting their minds. People's use of alcohol, illegal drugs, and anything else that promises to relieve the pressure is on the rise. The spirit of fear, anxiety, and panic is ruthless, even deadly, in our society.

WHAT BETTER WAY TO ALIENATE PEOPLE FROM GOD AND DESTROY THEM THAN TO USE THE DIRECT ACCESS OF DIGITAL AVENUES SUCH AS SMART DEVICES, COMPUTERS, AND TELEVISIONS TO DISSEMINATE FEAR?

A DARK VISION OF THE FUTURE

I became aware of the spiritual threat associated with the unchecked use of technology several years ago when I was awakened one night by the Holy Spirit to arise and pray. When I got up out of bed, laid my head on top of my Bible, and closed my eyes, I received a spiritual vision of the future. I saw masses of people suddenly being inundated by spirits of fear, panic, frustration, anger, and division. Millions of them were born-again believers who not only had been negatively affected by demonic powers but also had been *infected* by them. When I questioned how these ungodly spirits had gained access, I was shocked by the answer. These spirits were flooding into people's homes through their television sets, computers, and smart devices. As a result, masses of born-again believers had unwittingly become prey to the sinister plot of the enemy.

When I inquired further concerning what I was seeing, the Holy Spirit indicated, "Mark, you are witnessing the setup of the fall of the entire nation because of people's inability to recognize what is occurring between the digital and spiritual worlds." He continued, "You must warn My people!" When the Holy Spirit revealed what was occurring, I immediately alerted my family and our church. In the following months, I started sounding the alarm. Warning the church at large about this situation is one of the reasons I wrote this book.

Even now, entire households across the nation are unknowingly being infiltrated by ungodly spirits. Young people are being overcome by fear.

Research shows that nearly 34% of U.S. adults ages 18 to 64 will develop an anxiety disorder at least once in their lives. Data also reveals that anxiety disorders are the most common mental disorders among today's adolescents in the U.S., with approximately 32% of 13 to 17-year-olds having met the criteria for an anxiety disorder at least one point in their lives.[20]

While there are various issues that may cause anxiety in the lives of young people, including medical causes and traumatic incidents, I believe

20. Richard Scheffler et al., "The Anxious Generation: Causes and Consequences of Anxiety Disorder Among Young Americans: Preliminary Findings," Policy Brief, Berkeley Institute for the Future of Young Americans, July 2018, 1, https://gspp.berkeley.edu/assets/uploads/page/Policy_Brief_Final_071618.pdf.

social media has been a significant contributor to the rising prevalence of anxiety because of the fear-creators in the media. Additionally, many parents mistakenly believe that their children cease to be influenced by the content of their electronic devices the moment the devices are turned off. But we must realize that ungodly spirits can remain in a home long after cell phones and iPads are powered down. Their assignment? Interrupting and infecting children's rest with seemingly unexplainable nightmares and, worse, ungodly passions, appetites, and desires that no child should have to encounter, much less entertain.

OBSERVING OUR WORLD

Carefully open your eyes and ears to the world around you. The next time you are in your car or walking through a shopping area, take note of what you see and hear. After the Lord opened my eyes to what was happening, I started noticing things to which most people have grown accustomed, even if they don't realize it.

While driving along the road, I notice people in their cars screaming at their radios. I hear young people repeating demonic talking points set to a beat as they drive their vehicles. I also see young people walking with earphones jammed in their ears, listening to blasts of music. Most of them don't seem happy. Instead, their eyes and faces are filled with anger, rage, and fear. Many of them almost look like they are under a spell.

As I wait in airports to catch flights, I see people congregated around television monitors that are reporting on the latest crisis or scandal. People are being influenced by the voices of evil spirits that are now governing the spiritual frequencies of the air.

When I fly on airplanes and dine in restaurants, I hear people repeating the same biased talking points, parroting what they have heard or seen through toxic media streams—demonic incantations in concert.

Depression, despair, anger, and frustration share a common denominator: all of these emotions are rooted in or related to people's fear caused by various negative influences, such as hopelessness, rejection, or failure for which a person has no meaningful support.

According to the World Health Organization (WHO), "Suicide remains one of the leading causes of death worldwide.... Every year, more people die due to suicide than HIV, malaria or breast cancer—or war, and homicide. In 2019, more than 700,000 people died by suicide: one in every 100 deaths."[21] Media reports of suicides by celebrities can lead to a rise in the number of suicides due to imitation or "copycat" deaths, especially if the media accounts describe the particular methods of suicide.[22]

If it's true that "the devil is in the details," he is having a heyday!

RECLAIMING SPIRITUAL TERRITORY

The good news is that we do not have to remain unwitting victims of these ungodly spirits. An awakening is occurring in the church. God's people are being alerted and stirred to recognize the devil's plot. Christian leaders from around the world are sounding the alarm, and men and women of God are raising a standard. The Lord is building an army of savvy, presence-of-God-driven believers who are slamming shut these demonic gates and teaching others to do the same.

To clarify, technology itself is not the problem. The issue is our lack of discernment and discipline when using it. Our eyes must be opened to the danger. We can no longer allow the enemy to have free, unchecked access to our lives or to the lives of our children. We can no longer permit the enemy to use what God intended for our good to facilitate evil and spread fear and panic. In Jesus's name, we can reclaim our spiritual rights over the territory of technology, but it will require vigilance, education, and our support of one another.

TECHNOLOGY ITSELF IS NOT THE PROBLEM. THE ISSUE IS OUR LACK OF DISCERNMENT AND DISCIPLINE WHEN USING IT.

21. "One in 100 Deaths Is by Suicide," World Health Organization, news release, June 17, 2021, https://www.who.int/news/item/17-06-2021-one-in-100-deaths-is-by-suicide.
22. See, for example, "Association Between Suicide Reporting in the Media and Suicide: Systematic Review and Meta-Analysis," The BMJ, March 18, 2020, https://www.bmj.com/content/368/bmj.m575.

GOD USED A PANDEMIC

What the enemy meant for evil, God has used as a means to bless us. When the pandemic hit California, where I live, it forced Christian leaders and many other believers there to take a closer look at social media. Once leaders realized they could not hold in-person meetings at their churches during lockdowns and quarantines, they suddenly found themselves using social media and video conferencing platforms—whether through computers at their offices or through smartphones at their kitchen tables—to communicate with and calm their congregations. The same scenario was repeated throughout the nation and around the world. Pastors who had never before considered using technology as a means of sharing the power of God's peace and hope were suddenly forced to do so.

Within days of the initial lockdown, social media platforms like Facebook, YouTube, Instagram, and Twitter were flooded with posts and videos from pastors and their congregations spreading messages of faith over fear, hope over hopelessness, and the power of God to preserve those who are His. It was as if an "Internet revival" began to spread like wildfire. Millions who had been abused by fear through their televisions and smartphones were suddenly powering on to access faith and hope. While the media fired up their fear-mongering machines, born-again, Spirit-filled believers started to stoke the fires of the Holy Spirit!

Within ninety days, for perhaps the first time in technological history, the devil suddenly had genuine competition—so much so that the social media giants had to adjust their algorithms against the church and its spiritual warriors. As a result, the gospel of faith, hope, and peace began to flood these social media streams, combating and, in some cases, canceling fear's assignment in people's lives.

People who had never even gone to church started to listen in. While, previously, they had searched for the latest fear-mongering news story, they were now searching for somebody, anybody, who was sharing a message of peace and power over fear. Where fear had once moved to and fro with little or no opposition, a "new Sheriff" was in town. Discussions began to pop up all over social media about how it was time to "reclaim the territory" for God's kingdom. The demonic powers were terrified, and they still are. Why? Because the church has been awakened. And the fight continues!

OPEN THE FLOODGATES OF HEAVEN!

You might be wondering how we can reclaim the atmosphere—literal and figurative—for the kingdom of God. How do we evict fear, anxiety, and panic from the airwaves and replace them with God's peace, hope, and joy? I am convinced that recognizing where these fear-inducing spirits come from and what they have been doing in our lives is half the battle. If we are going to defeat tormenting spirits, we must identify the various channels they have been using to access our lives, and then shut them off. I am also convinced that the Holy Spirit is reawakening our spiritual discernment and our discipline to enable us to do this.

Believers must learn to stop feasting on fear and start feeding on faith through the Word of God and prayer. As I mentioned earlier, there's enough fear being spread via technology to infect entire nations. But the Bible assures us that all the fear the devil can generate stands no chance against the faith of God's people:

> For every child of God defeats this evil world, and we achieve this victory through our faith. And who can win this battle against the world? Only those who believe that Jesus is the Son of God.
>
> (1 John 5:4–5 NLT)

As we close off demonic access, let us also open the floodgates of heaven through praise, worship, and prayer! Let us reclaim and retake territory for the kingdom by preaching the gospel of peace through every form of technology available to us. Fear can be stripped of its power at the mere mention of faith in God's promises.

Jesus declared, "*I will give you the keys of the kingdom of heaven; whatever you bind on earth will be bound in heaven, and whatever you loose on earth will be loosed in heaven*" (Matthew 16:19 NIV). The metaphor is clear! Christ has given us the authority and power to bind and loose, open and close doors, and establish a foothold in the enemy's territory for advancing God's kingdom.

"*Lift up your gates, ye princes, and be ye lifted up, ye everlasting doors; and the king of glory shall come in*" (Psalm 24:7 BST). As Christian leaders awaken to the hour in which we are living, God will empower them to open the gates that were once shut against the kingdom so that the King of glory will come in. Glory gates will open, and the earth will tremble, allowing us to flood the world with the gospel message.

REPLACE NEGATIVE, FEARFUL INFLUENCES

People of God, blow the trumpet and sound the alarm! (See Joel 2:1.) We must replace negative, demonic words and images with positive, heavenly words and images. In my household, we removed every secular news network from our television sets and smart devices. News broadcasts through which we sensed fear and frustration being spread are no longer anywhere to be found in our home or automobiles. What did we do? We substituted them with programming like our own WestCoast Church ROKU and YouTube channels and our WestCoast Church super app. We subscribed to Christian networks like Daystar, TBN, Kenneth Copeland's Victory Channel, and others of like precious faith. In short, we subscribe to ministries that bless our family and fill our home with faith, spiritual strength, and peace. We do this to create, welcome, and celebrate an environment for heaven and its angels.

As for entertainment, we found clean, peace-filled programming on both Christian and secular networks. We also returned to watching some of the old black-and-white movies that showcase morality and peace over immorality and fear. To be clear, I am not trying to tell you what to do in relation to watching particular news programs and entertainment. But I am strongly urging you to wake up to Satan's tactics; stop the flow of fear into your eye gates, ear gates, and household; and increase the flow of faith and peace into every space of your life. I am asking you to carefully consider what you are allowing to enter your mind and heart, and to think about how it is affecting you in your relationship with God and others.

WAKE UP TO SATAN'S TACTICS; STOP THE FLOW OF FEAR INTO YOUR EYE GATES, EAR GATES, AND HOUSEHOLD; AND INCREASE THE FLOW OF FAITH AND PEACE INTO EVERY SPACE OF YOUR LIFE.

AN OUTPOURING IS COMING

Today, we have an unprecedented opportunity to expand the kingdom of God. An unparalleled outpouring of the Holy Spirit is imminent in America and the rest of the world. Let me challenge you to review this chapter again and to prayerfully take notes. Identify the places where ungodly spirits may have gained access to your life and home. Set aside time to review every device in your home and automobile for the content and atmosphere that you are taking in through it. In addition, check your children's phones and games, because your children are most vulnerable to such influences. Once you have identified those sources of demonic access, shut the gates to them! Consider having a family meeting concerning the changes you've decided to make in order to change the atmosphere of your family life for the better.

As you make the hard decisions to eliminate the influence of detrimental words and images, you will be surprised at the difference you sense in your life and in your home. People have told me that when they identified ungodly influences in their homes and followed through by shutting those destructive gates, the spiritual atmosphere was renewed to such an extent that it felt like they had remodeled their entire houses! Husbands and wives have reported experiencing a peace of mind they had not enjoyed in years. Entire families have gone from experiencing nightmares to receiving dreams and visitations from God's Spirit. Business owners and employees have said that it felt like the clutter in their minds had been removed, releasing them to accomplish more than ever before.

In coming chapters, you will discover more ways to become free from fear and experience a life that is filled with peace and fueled with power. It simply requires faith and the courage to do what must be done. Decide today, right now, that you are ready for positive change. Guard your ear gates and eye gates, and then witness what God does. Get ready to watch fear flee!

THE NARROW PATH FACE-OFF: A CLOSE ENCOUNTER OF THE COURAGEOUS KIND

"I've learned that fear limits you and your vision. It serves as
blinders to what may be just a few steps down the road for you.
The journey is valuable, but believing in your talents,
your abilities, and your self-worth can empower you to walk
down an even brighter path. Transforming fear into freedom—
how great is that?"
—*Soledad O'Brien*[23]

Any real fisherman will tell you that if you truly love the sport of fishing, it is sometimes necessary for you to grab your gear and go where no man (or woman) has gone before! That is, if you want to earn a special place on the wall at your favorite bait-and-tackle store, where others can see a photo of you and the trophy-sized fish you paid the price to locate and catch.

23. "Soledad O'Brien Quotes," https://www.brainyquote.com/quotes/soledad_obrien_648651.

Such was the case for me on a beautiful, cloudy day in Stockton, California, when I set out by myself to do a little salmon fishing. The word on the street was that the bigger fish were running upstream in one of the larger tributaries flowing out of the High Sierras. So, I grabbed my lures and bait and set off on my adventure.

When I arrived at my chosen location, pulled out my gear, and looked around, I was mesmerized by both the beauty of the stream and the old rustic bridge that spanned across it. The scene was breathtaking.

However, like most avid fishermen, I was more concerned about where I would find the fish than I was about the beauty of the landscape. Without lingering long, I set off across the rickety bridge, carefully watching each step so as not to fall through the old wooden slats beneath my feet and plunge into the river. The route was risky but necessary if I wanted to catch a glimpse of where those salmon might be hiding.

A NARROW, WELL-USED PATH

Looking down from the bridge, I could see the ice-cold water rushing over the river rocks and huge boulders that served to form the shallows leading to some deeper areas where the fish might be. I took off my sunglasses, and, as my eyes adjusted to the light, I started to capture the outline and reflections of several awe-inspiring fish as they swam in harmony just beneath the currents of the stream. I could hardly wait to get my line on the water!

However, as I looked more closely, I noticed that there was one problem: the fish, a little bit smarter than the average fisherman, had swum up to a place just beneath the bridge where they were schooled together in about four feet of water, just outside the rays of the sun peeking through the clouds.

I scanned the landscape that sloped down to the water and knew that a challenge awaited me. To get to where the fish were, I would have to slide about twenty-five feet down the side of that riverbank until I reached a narrow, worn path—made by one of the local mountain critters—that rested right alongside the river. "Easy enough," I reasoned.

I walked back across the bridge, picked up my gear, and headed toward what looked like the best place to descend. As I went, I gave myself a mental pep talk: "Okay, Mark, no worries! Remember, you've done this sort of thing before. Sit down, push off, and slide down this steep embankment on the seat of your britches to the tiny trail, and you are there. After all, the worst thing that could happen is that you would slide a little bit too fast and too far, leading to a swim in the ice-cold water!"

So, with a combination of faith, courage, and a little bit of stupidity, I slid down the hill toward the stream like a toboggan gliding down a snow-packed hill. Seconds later, I felt my feet catch just enough of the narrow trail to stop myself. *Relief*—I had made it. I was safe! Now it was time to fish.

WITH A COMBINATION OF FAITH, COURAGE, AND A LITTLE BIT OF STUPIDITY, I SLID DOWN THE HILL TOWARD THE STREAM LIKE A TOBOGGAN GLIDING DOWN A SNOW-PACKED HILL.

WHOSE PATH IS IT?

While standing on the narrow trail that rested at the bottom of the steep ridge overlooking the river, I was slightly amused to see how thin the path was. Whatever or whoever used this well-traveled trail couldn't be much larger than a squirrel or, at most, a bobcat.

A chill ran up my spine as my mind suddenly started to conjure up images of a brown bear coming down the fragile path in order to do its own salmon-fishing. Then I began to laugh out loud and talk to myself again, as if to keep myself company. "Mark, to travel down this path, a bear would have to be quite gifted—skillful enough to walk on a tightwire or ride a bicycle!" I tried to work off my concerns by concentrating on the fishing and shrugging off the idea of a bear joining me at my fishing spot.

However, as I stood there, I couldn't help beginning to wonder again, "What in the world could be using this tiny path? It is really too narrow for a larger animal. After all, I barely have room to stand on this thing!"

I was carefully working to maintain my balance as I stood on the slender path and fished when I suddenly heard something behind me. Quietly, I set my fishing rod down on the ground and slowly lowered my sunglasses from the crown of my nose to get a better look at what was coming toward me from a distance.

I was pleasantly surprised and gratefully relieved to discover it wasn't a brown bear on a bicycle or a bobcat. "So, that's who this path belongs to," I said. Moving along the trail was the cutest little bushy gray-and-red squirrel I had ever seen.

At first, I smiled and thought to myself, "He must be following me!" But then I noticed that the squirrel wasn't traveling at a friendly, leisurely pace. He was running up that path toward me like something was after him. He was *hauling*!

As I watched the animal sprint down the slope of the narrow path toward me, I was a little confused about what would occur when he arrived at the spot where I was standing. Surely, he would stop—if for no other reason than out of fear of my presence. Perhaps he would run up the embankment to get around me.

But he wasn't slowing down—he was speeding up. "Yikes!" I thought to myself. "I am not backing down! I am much larger than this guy. He is a squirrel, and I am a human being. It's my path today, not his!" As he drew even closer, I tried to convince myself, "Okay, I am sure he's going to slow down, stop, and then run up the hill around me. Or maybe he'll get scared, turn around, and run back the other way."

In what felt like the very last moment, the little guy finally put on his brakes, slid sideways, and came to a screeching halt. I exhaled and thought, "Thank You, Jesus!"

UP CLOSE AND PERSONAL

Now that we were close enough to really observe each other, something occurred between that squirrel and me that you might see in a Walt Disney movie. As the squirrel worked to catch his breath—and we both attempted to figure out what would happen next—our eyes met. I felt like he was staring me down or sizing me up. For me, it was as if my eyes had a camera lens, and it had zoomed in for an "up close and personal" view of the animal's eyes.

What followed will forever be captured in my memory. The squirrel shifted his little head to glance behind him. Then he quickly looked back toward me as if he were trying to decide which was the greater "Goliath threat": whatever was chasing him or the large guy standing on his path.

Again, his wide little eyes met mine, and mine met his. Suddenly, it was as if he went from being a little furry squirrel to a two-thousand-pound bull! He leaned forward, repositioned his forehead in a plow-through stance, and started scratching the path. He snorted and kicked dust beneath him as if he were preparing to rush a matador in the ring. But why should I be concerned? I smiled as I remembered that the average California grey squirrel is only about two pounds.

But when he maintained his stance, I thought, "This can't be happening to me. Am I really about to be run over or, worse, gored, by a tiny, two-pound critter?" He looked like his mind was made up. Apparently, he had concluded that whatever was behind him presented more of a danger than I did.

I refound my courage. I wasn't moving—no matter what.

So much for my resolve. Like a rocket blasting off a launching pad or a track star dashing off the starting block, that little furry creature barreled straight toward me. Milliseconds later, I shot upward as the propulsion from the impact sent my body over the five-foot embankment and into the ice-cold stream! As I entered the water, I heard a splash, followed by the deafening sound of being submerged.

When I popped my head up out of the water, my senses seemed to be on overdrive as every hair on my body stood on end from that frigid dunking. There I was, wading in several feet of water, paddling against the current with my hands. Meanwhile, the little creature continued along his merry way down the path to freedom, as if he had just won the Indianapolis 500.

The score was clear: furry creature, ten; brave fisherman who had dared to stand in his path, zero.

I broke out into laughter as I struggled to pull myself out of the stream and up onto the bank again. At that point, the only remaining evidence of our close encounter of the courageous kind was a bushy tail disappearing down the trail and a bit of dust lingering behind it.

PRINCIPLES OF COURAGE

When I drove home that night, I began to laugh out loud again and again as I recalled, in slow motion, vivid images of our confrontation. I thought to myself, "What in the world happened?" From my perspective, I had failed in my face-off with a tiny creature! Evidently, from the little guy's perspective, whatever was behind him was far more threatening to him than I was, so he wasn't going to let me stop him.

Even more amusing was my memory of the little critter's scowling face as he scratched the ground, huffing and puffing and preparing to shoot straight through me. That sight alone should have been enough for me to have said, "Hey, give me a second, and I'll move out of your way!" To this day, I can remember the look in that squirrel's beady little eyes, as if he were trying to say, "Big man, if you don't get out of my way, I will claw and plow my way right over you! It's your choice. But it is happening!"

Then I had a powerful epiphany. As tiny as that squirrel was, he had found within him a courage great enough to overcome the massive obstacle that stood in his path—namely, me! The little guy hadn't chased me into the water because I was smaller than he was but because his courage was larger than the situation. After all, it was his path. He had succeeded in reclaiming that trail because I represented what stood between him (and possibly his family) and his preservation—his very future. Wow!

Later, when I arrived back home, I sat down at the desk in my office, picked up a freshly sharpened pencil and a crisp, white pad of paper, and jotted down some notes. I have since refined and expanded on those thoughts, adding insights that I have gleaned along the way, resulting in the following points:

1. By the Spirit, we carry within us the ability to turn natural fear into supernatural power—a power that can overcome everything that opposes God's plan and purpose for our lives. All we need do is tap into that power to take hold of what is rightfully ours in Him.

2. The path that leads to true freedom belongs to those brave enough to lay claim to it.

3. It's not how wide the path, but rather how courageous the heart, that determines how large the victory.

4. Authentic freedom is purchased with the currency of faith, courage, and tenacity.

5. Determination fueled by desperation releases the capacity to defeat or remove anything or anyone that stands between us and all that belongs to our future.

6. Faith and fear cannot occupy the same space.

WITH GOD-GIVEN COURAGE AND TENACITY, WE CAN BOLDLY LAY CLAIM TO ALL THAT IS RIGHTFULLY OURS IN HIM.

COURAGE TO OVERCOME DOUBT AND FEAR

My encounter with that determined squirrel was only a small incident. However, it reminds me of how powerful our God-given faith is and how important it is to recall the above principles of courage when we face large obstacles in our lives, especially as we struggle with doubt and fear. Theodore Roosevelt said, "It is only through labor and painful effort, by grim energy and resolute courage, that we move on to better things."[24] Tackling our trepidation takes determined courage—but, remember, that

---

24. "Theodore Roosevelt Quotes," https://www.theodorerooseveltcenter.org/Learn-About-TR/TR-Quotes?page=92.

kind of courage comes from the power of God's voice and presence in our lives.

The Bible is filled with inspiring stories about men and women who felt weak, insignificant, and, yes, fearful, but who discovered that God transforms weaknesses into strength and fear into faith. Gideon, who became a judge in Israel, was such an individual who felt engulfed in weakness and apprehension. Considering Gideon's later exploits, it's hard to picture him as a downbeat, skeptical man. We usually think of him as his Hebrew name describes him: "feller (i.e. warrior)" or "hewer,"[25] as of wood, who cuts down or breaks into pieces. We envision him as a mighty fighter who destroyed the altar of Baal and, in the end, led a small troop of only three hundred men to victory over tens of thousands of marauding Midianites.

However, at the beginning, Gideon gave no intimation of his courage and faith. Instead, when the angel of the Lord appeared to him to tell him that he would fight against the Midianite army, he was pessimistic and cynical.

> *The Israelites did evil in the eyes of the Lord, and for seven years he gave them into the hands of the Midianites.... Midian so impoverished the Israelites that they cried out to the Lord for help.... The angel of the Lord came and sat down under the oak in Ophrah that belonged to Joash the Abiezrite, where his son Gideon was threshing wheat in a winepress to keep it from the Midianites. When the angel of the Lord appeared to Gideon, he said, "The Lord is with you, mighty warrior." "Pardon me, my lord," Gideon replied, "but if the Lord is with us, why has all this happened to us? Where are all his wonders that our ancestors told us about when they said, 'Did not the Lord bring us up out of Egypt?' But now the Lord has abandoned us and given us into the hand of Midian." The Lord turned to him and said, "Go in the strength you have and save Israel out of Midian's hand. Am I not sending you?" "Pardon me, my lord," Gideon replied, "but how can I save Israel? My clan is the weakest in Manasseh, and I am the least in my family."* (Judges 6:1, 6, 11–15 NIV)

---

25. *Strong's Exhaustive Concordance of the Bible*, #G1439, https://www.bibletools.org/index.cfm/fuseaction/Lexicon.show/ID/H1439/Gid%60own.htm.

Gideon initially doubted or disbelieved everything the angel told him. And even when he was convinced that he had seen an angel, he assumed the worst, retaining a fearful spirit right up to the hour of battle with Midian. In short, Gideon became a great hero, but he was not a great hero at the start.

Talk about someone having deep-rooted feelings of inadequacy—that was Gideon! But note what God told him in Judges 6:16: "*The* Lord *answered, 'I will be with you, and you will strike down all the Midianites, leaving none alive'*" (NIV).

What's interesting about Gideon's conversation with God is that the Lord didn't initially bring up the subject of an army or the number of warriors that would be needed to face the Midianites. When He said, "*I will be with you,*" I think He was trying to communicate something powerful to Gideon: "When I am with you, nothing else really matters." In other words, if God is for you and within you, who or what can stand against you? (See, for example, Romans 8:31.)

No matter how small or weak you might feel, the God who lives within you is more powerful than any obstacle in your way or any enemy that dares to come against you. It is on this truth that you can base your courage.

Another great biblical figure of courage is Deborah, one of the most influential women in the Old Testament, who was a prophetess, judge, and warrior. She was used by the Lord to lead worship and to speak to God's people on His behalf in difficult times. Considering how unusual it was in the culture of that day for women to be leaders, and the resistance she might have encountered, Deborah must have had supernatural faith in order to obey God's call on her life.

I imagine it also must have required spiritual courage for Deborah to lead not only a commander but also a whole army in battle. Yet that is exactly what she did. We read about this story in Judges 4:

> *Again the Israelites did evil in the eyes of the* Lord, *now that Ehud* [another judge of Israel] *was dead. So the* Lord *sold them into the hands of Jabin king of Canaan, who reigned in Hazor. Sisera, the commander of his army, was based in Harosheth Haggoyim. Because he had nine hundred chariots fitted with iron and had cruelly oppressed*

the Israelites for twenty years, they cried to the LORD for help. Now Deborah, a prophet, the wife of Lappidoth, was leading Israel at that time. She held court under the Palm of Deborah between Ramah and Bethel in the hill country of Ephraim, and the Israelites went up to her to have their disputes decided. She sent for Barak son of Abinoam from Kedesh in Naphtali and said to him, "The LORD, the God of Israel, commands you: 'Go, take with you ten thousand men of Naphtali and Zebulun and lead them up to Mount Tabor. I will lead Sisera, the commander of Jabin's army, with his chariots and his troops to the Kishon River and give him into your hands.'" (Judges 4:1–7 NIV)

Deborah's faith-infused fearlessness was so powerful that Barak, the male commander of the army, told her, with regard to battling Sisera: *"If you go with me, I will go; but if you don't go with me, I won't go"* (Judges 4:8 NIV). Interestingly, in the next verse, Deborah agreed to go to battle with Barak and his troops but with a major clause: *"'Certainly I will go with you,' said Deborah. 'But because of the course you are taking, the honor will not be yours, for the LORD will deliver Sisera into the hands of a woman'"* (Judges 4:9 NIV).

Once more, the courage that inspired and drove Deborah to lead Barak and his men into battle was not her own. It was the supernatural courage of her Lord and Creator—the God of Abraham, Isaac, and Jacob—that burned deep within the recesses of her spirit. Her example must have made even the most valiant Israelite warrior take notice and do a spiritual inventory of his own life. I believe that it was Deborah's courage that gave the Israelites clarity, strength, and courage to defeat Sisera. The Lord was using this mighty woman of God to lead the Israelite army to victory in order to fulfill His will.

The real clincher in this story is that, while the Israelites were battling Sisera, God raised up another woman by the name of Jael to finish the job. The Bible says she drove a tent peg through Sisera's temple after he fled the battle and was trying to hide from the Israelite army. (See Judges 4:16–21.)

There are powerful lessons to be learned from the lives of Gideon and Deborah. First and foremost, we see that supernatural courage transcends background, stature, and gender. It is one of the attributes that we inherit from our divine Creator as His born-again children. In fact, I love how the apostle Paul, who wrote two thirds of the New Testament, confirms this truth in Galatians 3:26–29:

> So in Christ Jesus you are all children of God through faith, for all of you who were baptized into Christ have clothed yourselves with Christ. There is neither Jew nor Gentile, neither slave nor free, nor is there male and female, for you are all one in Christ Jesus. If you belong to Christ, then you are Abraham's seed, and heirs according to the promise. (NIV)

Your difficult family background, physical weakness, emotional pain, gender, or anything else you think is hindering you from overcoming your fears is no match for the courage you can receive from God to rise up in newfound strength, peace, and purpose. Similar to the little squirrel in the story, you have a unique, God-given path. It's your route, and it will enable you to fulfill your divine destiny. But do not be surprised if your journey is blocked by unanticipated resistance. In moments of opposition, you might become unnerved, but God will convert your anxiety into peace, your weakness into strength, and your fear into faith.

Mark Twain had vague but ever-present guilt and fears. It was as if Twain did not trust life itself and always sought ways to defend himself from its dangers and unknowns. But he learned to overcome his ingrained habit of discouragement and fear and to see the world as more of a friendly place than a treacherous one. He said, "Courage is resistance to fear, mastery of fear—not absence of fear."[26] And Muhammad Ali said, "He who is not courageous enough to take risks will accomplish nothing in life."[27]

IN MOMENTS OF OPPOSITION, YOU MIGHT BECOME UNNERVED, BUT GOD WILL CONVERT YOUR ANXIETY INTO PEACE, YOUR WEAKNESS INTO STRENGTH, AND YOUR FEAR INTO FAITH.

---

26. "Courage Is Resistance to Fear, Mastery of Fear—Not Absence of Fear," Quote Investigator, https://quoteinvestigator.com/2019/11/26/courage-fear/.
27. "He Who Is Not Courageous Enough To Take Risks Will Accomplish Nothing in Life," https://quoteinvestigator.com/2019/06/23/risks/.

So, whenever a dangerous blockade is erected in your life, remember that some decisions are required of you. Will you choose courage or fear? Faith or pessimism? Serenity or anxiety?

Choose God's courage over your fears and stay the course. Turning back is not an option. The trail has a purpose, but it may not always be smooth traveling. Sometimes the road ahead is not yet visible, and we don't know what to expect. But as we keep going, the path clears, and the fog of life dissipates in the light of God's presence.

Remember, when God says, "I will be with you" and gives you His courage, the size of the opposition suddenly no longer matters. Don't hold back but keep moving ahead. It's your path. Take it. Your future—and the future of others—may depend on it!

PART TWO

SOURCES OF FEAR

IRRATIONAL FEAR:
IT'S ALL ABOUT PERCEPTION

"It is the mind, that maketh good or ill,
that maketh wretched or happy, rich or poor."
—*Edmund Spenser*[28]

Our world faces unprecedented challenges that are producing a great sense of uneasiness and alarm around the globe. However, many people worldwide are also contending with fears that are not based on reality or facts but are a result of their imaginations creating false narratives. As I described earlier, such fears are unnatural, irrational, and exaggerated. Individuals are afraid of things that aren't true or that exhibit no real evidence of being a threat to them. Irrational fears interrupt people's everyday lives and prevent them from engaging in new experiences. Most of all, they keep people from the peace and purpose that God offers us in Christ.

---

28. Edmund Spenser, *The Faerie Queene*. Lightly modernized from the original. Please see Goodreads, "Edmund Spenser/Quotes/Quotable Quotes," https://www.goodreads.com/quotes/8741691-it-is-the-mynd-that-maketh-good-or-ill-that.

We can all be victims of irrational fear at one time or another. To give a simple but graphic illustration, the following is a story about how, when I was a young man, I allowed my imagination to go into overdrive.

THE BEAST IN THE FOREST

Anyone who has spent time in the vastness of a forest can tell you that the wilderness can be a scary place, especially at night. The dangers inherent in a forest were drilled and instilled into me from the time I was a child. My uncles on my mother's side of the family were avid hunters. They were not casual hunters who sported the latest fashions from the local outdoor outlet store. Nor were they inexperienced hunters who sat in their safe camps, never venturing more than a few hundred feet from their base or the nearest roads. Instead, my kind soaked their clothes in deer urine and pine leaves before hiking miles into the forest, and they didn't come out for days. These guys were the real thing, and they related many gripping accounts of their confrontations with grizzly bears, cougars, wildcats, and mountain lions. They had the photos, mounted animal heads, and full-body animal mountings to prove it!

So, by the time I was old enough to follow in their footsteps, I was not only fully outfitted with the equipment and weapons needed for a hunting trip, but my imagination was also filled with dozens of those mesmerizing stories, along with the terrorizing images they evoked. (I'm sure my uncles embellished most of the stories to keep their young nephews and nieces on the edge of their seats. It worked!)

On one of my earliest real hunting expeditions, I was with a group of guys that included my brother, Chuck, who was seven years older than I was. Chuck was enamored of everything about hunting that he and I had grown up hearing about. The previous year, we had hunted in the forest during the day, but this year would be different. We would awaken sometime after midnight, make our way up to the ridge of the mountain in the darkness, and wait until daybreak with nothing more than our rifles and flashlights. We needed to delay hunting until morning because hunting at night was not permitted.

This meant we would sit in our respective places waiting for the deer to come to us, rather than our going to them. It sounded like a great plan to me! Get up, get dressed, grab our gear, climb up the mountain, find a good spot to sit together in the exceedingly dark forest, and look for the sunrise.

There was one problem. I could have sworn I had heard my brother say we would go up the mountain *together*. Or, perhaps, I was thinking about that pitch-black forest, my mind had just *wanted* to hear it. On the night we left, when everyone was making final preparations for the trek, my brother said, "Okay, guys, we'll meet you back here at camp in a few hours. Good luck, and happy hunting!"

"Excuse me," I said. "I thought we were all going up the mountain together." One of the guys replied, "We did travel here together. But we're all hunting alone!" To which I replied (in my best masculine voice), "You mean, we're all going up the mountain our separate ways?"

As everyone else began walking off into the dark with their rifles over their shoulders, I heard someone answer, "Yes, sir! Pretty much." My brother added, "Guys, if anyone gets in trouble, fire off two or three shots and repeat until we find one another."

"You've got to be kidding!" I thought.

But, into the forest I went, taking a deep breath and reasoning, "If my brother can do it, and my uncles have done it a thousand times, I can do it too!" As I made my way, the sights and smells of the campfire and the rustling sounds that the other guys made as they pushed through the branches completely disappeared. Within a few moments, the only things I could hear were the noises of the forest. I directed the beam of my small flashlight toward every small sound I heard around me. I could feel my legs cramping and my lungs pumping, alerting me that I was ascending a steep mountain.

The dark forest seemed to get larger and denser as I climbed over boulders and massive logs. My heart beat fast, and my eyes labored to find a place where I could hide if needed.

Finally, I reached the ridge. I had thought the sun would be shining by now, but it was still very dark. Sighing, I realized that I had gone up the mountain in such a hurry that I had arrived about two hours before sunup.

As my eyes searched my surroundings, I located a place to rest between a huge boulder and a fairly large pine tree. Carefully and quietly, I sat down, trying not to make any noise, hoping not to scare away any approaching deer or give away my location to other animals that might be around.

I clicked the switch of my flashlight to see if I could read the time on my watch, but the battery was dead! My heart rate sped up again as I realized I had no way of illuminating the area if I heard a wild animal approaching me. Within seconds, many of the images my imagination had created from the stories my uncles had told crowded into my mind.

Just then, I heard a noise that seemed to come from the right of where I was sitting. It was moving in my direction with the sound of "crunch, crunch, crunch." I sat perfectly still but used every muscle in my eyes to try to see through the darkness, craving to catch a glimpse of whatever was making that sound.

The noise seemed to be getting closer, and I turned my head toward it. A black or brown bear, perhaps? I suddenly remembered the story one of my uncles had told about his confrontation with a six-hundred-pound bear. Even after he shot it, the animal had continued charging him until he finally killed it within feet of where he was standing! I also recalled the following warning from my uncles: "Marky, if you ever find yourself face-to-face with these monsters, don't try to outrun them. They can run uphill at around forty miles an hour like they have four-wheel drive!" One uncle had talked about a buddy who had been mauled and dragged for thirty feet by a bear before being left to die. Thinking about a bear's ability to run up a hill at forty miles an hour left my heart thumping wildly.

> **JUST THEN, I HEARD A NOISE THAT SEEMED TO COME FROM THE RIGHT OF WHERE I WAS SITTING. IT WAS MOVING IN MY DIRECTION WITH THE SOUND OF "CRUNCH, CRUNCH, CRUNCH."**

The forest suddenly seemed to go silent, and my eyes scanned the area for any signs of the beast I had just heard, which was likely tracking me.

Then I caught sight of a huge figure about sixty-five feet away. I was able to discern the shadowy outline of the beast's enormous head and body. It was lying down as if waiting for daybreak—and its breakfast.

I froze. If I fired my gun in the air, would the sound chase the bear away? Then I remembered these words of my uncle "Bubbo": "Marky, some of these bears have no fear of guns, and, unfortunately, they won't fall with the first shot if you do hit them. And whatever you do, don't try to shoot them in the head. These animals are known to have extremely thick, hard skulls. If you miss them, or, worse, if you shoot them and make them mad, they're likely to catch you and toss you around the forest before killing and eating you!"

Still feeling paralyzed, I began praying under my breath, "Please, Lord, make this thing get up and go away!" As I prayed to God in one track of my mind, I talked to myself in another. "What is this thing waiting for? Is it playing with me? Does it want me to make the first move? Maybe I could slowly get up and move away downhill. But what if it starts to charge me? Or chases me downhill?"

I slowly brought my watch up to my right eye and squinted, attempting to use all the power of my night vision to see the time. The hour hand was at four and the minute hand was at twenty-two. It wasn't even four thirty yet! That meant I still had at least forty minutes before the sun would rise, bringing light to the forest.

Then the creature made another noise. It sounded as if it was either getting up or, at the very least, repositioning itself—hopefully not for an attack! But maybe it was resting and didn't even know I was there. After all, I hadn't made a sound, even when I would slowly move my arm up to my eyes to check the time. In my attempts to remain quiet, I had even been allowing mosquitoes to bite me without my moving a muscle.

I was sure I heard the beast taking slow and shallow breaths, as if it were waiting for me to move. I had only one option—outlast it, hoping it would eventually get up and go away. I continued to sit perfectly still in the dark, watching intently, but it was clear the animal wasn't budging. My mind seemed to kick into flight-for-life mode as I thought, "If you get up and attempt to slowly walk away, you might make it, although you would have to feel your way through a dark forest to get back to camp." Another part of me cautioned, "But Mark, you are no match for this animal! Remember? These beasts can run forty miles per hour!" In my head, my uncle's voice interrupted the other voices, saying, "Mark, whatever happens, do not try running away from these bears! They will catch you, maul you, and maybe eat you!"

Finally, the rays of the sun began penetrating the forest, revealing, in all its glory, what had filled me with dread for more than two hours.

Straight ahead of me, a gentle fawn rose to its feet.

All that worry over how to outsmart or outwait what I had thought was a massive bear had been in vain! I had allowed myself to be terrorized by a fawn that had found a resting place next to a thousand-pound, bear-shaped tree stump.

I burst out laughing. Not only had my fears been unwarranted, but they had also been extremely creative. Fear had awakened my imagination, inviting it to participate in conceiving a completely false scenario.

THE DANGER OF A FALSE NARRATIVE

My experience with the "monster fawn" gave me one of my first lessons about the ability of our imaginations to deceive us. The Roman philosopher Seneca expressed a vital truth when he said, "There are more things… likely to frighten us than there are to crush us; we suffer more often in imagination than in reality."[29]

As we briefly talked about in chapter 3, irrational fear is an extreme, unwarranted emotion linked to a specific object, event, or person. Irrational fears cause us to react to threats that do not exist. When we believe a falsehood, we often create and perpetuate a negative faith in a worst-case scenario that is groundless, unjustifiable, or absurdly ridiculous. We manufacture mental trip wires that lead us to attribute cause and effect to people's behavior or to events when they do not actually correspond. When not countered by godly reason and understanding, a false narrative can engender ungoverned fear.

---

29. Maria Popova, "A Stoic's Key to Peace of Mind: Seneca on the Antidote to Anxiety," *The Marginalian*, https://www.themarginalian.org/2017/08/27/seneca-anxiety/.

Millions of people are hurt more by the effects of their fictitious thoughts than they are by reality. False narratives create flawed thinking. This is why people are tormented by imagined fears of scenarios that will never come to pass. Many individuals also suffer from what their imaginations create out of past negative events that should no longer hold power over them.

God designed the human imagination for our good. Through our imaginations, we are able to conceive ideas and create things as a reflection of our having been created in God's image. We will talk further about this wonderful gift of the imagination later in the chapter. However, when the imagination is improperly applied, it can detour, distract, and debilitate us, causing us to suffer. In contrast, when we have a proper view of a situation based on what is actually occurring in our lives, and if we apply the truths of God's Word to that situation, we can arrive at a healthy, positive response.

MILLIONS OF PEOPLE ARE HURT MORE BY THE EFFECTS OF THEIR FICTITIOUS THOUGHTS THAN THEY ARE BY REALITY.

A VICTIM OF OTHERS' INSECURITIES

Most of us can remember a time when we failed to look at a situation closely enough, only to discover we had it completely wrong. This happens to many people in their interactions with others, resulting in friction, hurt feelings, bitterness, and broken relationships. If we are not careful, our imaginations can create such misunderstandings, or they may be caused by others projecting their own fears and insecurities on us.

Have you ever completely misjudged another person's motivations or attitudes and intensions toward you? Was that perception formed, at least in part, by other people's false impressions, which influenced you? I vividly recall a particular time when this happened to me in high school.

Like many testosterone-filled teenage boys, I had awkward moments when someone might have wondered if I was two cents short of a dollar! While those experiences were sorely embarrassing to me at the time, God has converted the painful experiences and memories into powerful life lessons that have helped me to grow into the person He intended me to be. In this situation when I was a teenager, the Holy Spirit taught me a lesson I would not soon forget. It was another clear illustration of the difference between perception and reality—and finding the wisdom to know the difference.

It all began on a beautiful, crisp fall morning. As usual, I arrived at my high school a little later than I should have. I headed toward the area where my friends congregated, the place where we usually met up for casual conversation and some girl-watching before classes began.

When I walked up to where everyone was standing around, one of my friends nodded at me and said, "Dude, did you hear? There's a new guy in school."

"Cool," I replied, and then asked, "Does anyone know him?"

Almost in unison, several of my friends nodded toward the direction of where this new boy was sitting. One of them replied, "No, but whoever he is, he's wearing some bad-boy-looking sunglasses and tennis shoes!" Another friend said, "Wow! Look at the size of that guy's arms! He's a pretty large dude. Maybe he's here to play football?"

"Who knows?" I said. "But I've got to get to class. If I'm late today, I'm going to be staying after school!"

Everyone laughed, saying, "You're always late, Filkey!"

"Yeah, I know," I admitted.

As I picked up my books and coat, one of my friends hit me on the shoulder and said, "You know what? That new guy hasn't stopped looking at you since you got here. Are you sure you don't know him?"

I laughed, saying, "What makes you think he has an issue with me?"

"Dude! Take a look! He hasn't stopped staring at you. He looks like he's just waiting for you to say something to him."

I looked across the schoolyard and tried to figure out why this guy was looking straight at me. Leaning forward, and believing I had his attention, I nodded my head at him as if to say, "What's up?" thinking he would most likely look away or back down. But, after a couple of minutes, it was evident he wasn't backing down. I could hardly believe it. My friends appeared to be right. This guy was calling me out. He wanted to fight me!

My heart raced, and I shouted, with the most challenging tone I could muster, "Hey, dude! What are you looking at?" His response? He appeared to calmly reposition himself on the edge of the bench where he was sitting, as if he were redirecting all of his attention toward me.

My friends began to egg me on, whispering, "Mark, you need to walk right over there and ask him what his problem is."

For one short moment, I had a tiny burst of sanity and intelligence mixed with a spoonful of common sense. I thought to myself, "If I go over to this guy, and he doesn't back down, I'm in trouble. He's huge. What if he does want to fight? This guy could kill me!"

About that time, one of my friends whispered, "Mark, look! He's getting up!"

In a knee-jerk reaction, I stood straight up, placed my hands at my sides, and tightened my chest, as if to say via body language, "Come on, then. Let's do this!" Prepping my mind for a fight, I told my friends, "No one looks at me like that and gets away with it. If this guy wants trouble, he's found it." Then I turned in toward the group and whispered, "You guys stay here. I'm going over there to find out what this guy's problem is."

I pulled up my pants, and, as my friends cheered me on, I boldly made my way across the schoolyard toward the place where the new guy was standing. However, just as I got about twenty-five feet from him, a classroom door just to the right of where he was standing opened. A teacher came out, placed her hand on his shoulder, and handed him a long white cane with a red tip on the end of it. He smiled, put his hand on her arm, and let her lead him into the classroom.

The door shut behind them, and I heard a sudden burst of laughter break out behind me. Recognizing their own flawed perception, my friends were on the ground in hysterics. As for me, I was stunned by what had just occurred. My friends had projected their insecurities on me, convincing me that I needed to defend myself. Even worse, I had officially been twenty-five feet away from starting a fight with a disabled young man who, I soon discovered, could hardly see or hear. My irrational fear had made a complete fool of me.

THE COMMUNICABLE DISEASE OF IRRATIONAL FEAR

I walked back across the courtyard toward my friends with a strange mixture of feelings, mostly relief and utter stupidity. Later, as I sat in my first class, something dawned on me. When I had arrived at school, I'd had no thought of getting into a confrontation. What's more, I probably wouldn't even have noticed that young man if my friends hadn't pointed him out to me. I hadn't originally been the one who thought he was giving me dirty looks. It was the guys I was hanging out with who had believed that. They had transferred their false perceptions to me. Unknowingly, I had fallen prey to irrational fear.

That day, I discovered a powerful truth: unnatural, irrational fear can be contagious. Anxiety and apprehension can be transmitted to others. This means that even if you do not have irrational fear now, you can catch it if you do not guard against it. Ungodly fears perpetuated by irrational thoughts are easily conveyed from one person to another. Such irrational fears are to the ungoverned soul what disease is to a vulnerable physical body.

In medical terminology, you could say that unfounded fears are "communicable." Through communication between people, fear and anxiety can be spiritually passed from one soul to another. Those who are carriers of fear and anxiety—the spiritually infectious—are, in many cases, unaware that they are imposing their particular negativities on others. I've known solid, born-again believers who, through their vulnerabilities, were unwittingly exposed to fear by another person and became anxious, exhibiting the same symptoms as that other person. They finally realized they had been infected by fears that weren't their own but had been imposed on them by powers of darkness. Once they realized what was happening and rejected the acquired fear, they were able to be set free from it.

EVEN IF YOU DO NOT HAVE IRRATIONAL FEAR NOW, YOU CAN CATCH IT IF YOU DO NOT GUARD AGAINST IT.

Fear is a poison that can spin even the most settled mind into a state of confusion. Clarence Jordan got it right when he said, "Fear is the polio of the soul which prevents our walking by faith."[30] When we cease walking by faith, according to God's confidence and courage—or when we have not yet learned to walk by faith—we can become susceptible to unnatural fears, which God never intended for us.

In chapter 3, we discussed how some irrational fears emerge as phobias, such as a fear of being out in public or a fear of being in a confined space. Another type of phobia is a fear of heights, which may cause someone to avoid driving over bridges or being in elevated places because they are afraid they will fall. Such phobias can control people, leaving them trapped in an unhealthy lifestyle. George Addair said, "Everything you've ever wanted is on the other side of fear."[31]

We may not immediately recognize various irrational fears that have been holding us back. It's important to take inventory of how our fears have been influencing us and affecting how we perceive situations and how we behave. When we take action to recognize and face our fears, we will be able to defeat them. Ignoring our fears will likely only accentuate them. In most cases, it is not really fear itself that is hindering us but rather the stories we have concocted that have led to the fears and that keep fueling them. False narratives are stealing our happiness, peace, and ability to release our potential.

As I've expressed previously, while there may be specific contributors to fear, such as negative life circumstances and thought patterns, much of our irrational fear ultimately comes from the devil. Satan and his minions, as is their habit, have taken a gift from God—healthy fear that protects us

---

30. "The Substance of Faith Quotes," Goodreads, https://www.goodreads.com/work/quotes/1392774-the-substance-of-faith-and-other-cotton-patch-sermons.
31. "George Addair/Quotes/Quotable Quote," Goodreads, https://www.goodreads.com/quotes/1216350-everything-you-ve-ever-wanted-is-on-the-other-side-of.

from danger—and deviously corrupted it, using it against us. They do this by inserting thoughts of encroaching disaster and doom into our minds. Behind the door of fear are the "What if?" questions that tie us in knots of terror. Unregenerate souls or, at least, unenlightened or unprepared souls are incredibly susceptible to the dangerous spiritual disease of irrational fear. It is a disorder that sets people's souls in a place of unease.

To better understand this phenomenon, let's look again at Paul's message to Timothy about fear:

> *Wherefore I put you in remembrance that you stir up the gift of God, which is in you by the putting on of my hands. For God has not given us the spirit of fear; but of power, and of love, and of a sound mind.*
>
> (2 Timothy 1:6–7 KJVER)

A spirit of fear *within* us in too great a degree exaggerates dangers that are *without*. The potential for fear resides in the mind, but the antidote to fear is the power of God, a courageous heart, and a godly outlook, all of which will give us victory over external circumstances.

The apostle Paul realized that most of the believers in the fledgling church of the first century faced similar trials and persecutions—internal and external—to those that he and his team encountered. Writing from prison, he reminded Timothy and the believers under his care of the spirit of faith living inside them and empowering them to overcome all fear.

Paul did what I am endeavoring to do with you right now—stir up your faith! He challenged Timothy to fan the flames of God's gifts residing within him. Paul also reminded Timothy of who he was in Christ. The God-given spirit of power, love, and a sound mind within Timothy would enable him to avoid being infected by an ungodly spirit of fear.

Today, we think we are under a deluge of adversity that tempts us to fear, but we need to consider what the early church had to endure. When we read passages such as the one from 1 Timothy above, we may forget that the men and women to whom the New Testament letters were written didn't just face the danger of persecution. They faced other types of peril as well. They had to deal with various debilitating and deadly diseases without the benefit of hospitals, doctors, or surgeons as we know them today. There was nothing like our modern-day pain relievers, vaccines, antibiotics, and other medicines. If there was an emergency, they couldn't call 911 or the fire department. Imagine if the latest outbreak of leprosy were just a few miles from where you lived or you a faced a natural disaster without any medical support.

The early believers also lived with other limitations. There were no advanced forms of transportation, such as automobiles, trains, and planes, that we can make use of today. There were no Christian television or radio networks, prayer lines on Christian websites or social media, or email newsletters coming from their favorite preachers to encourage them. Only a few people had direct access to written copies of the Old Testament, and no one had the complete New Testament to read for encouragement and prayer.

Much as we do today, the early Christians had to guard their minds and spirits against the fearful realities of their time, along with the irrational thoughts that bombarded their minds and emotions. Although they lacked the modern benefits I mentioned above, what they did have—and what we also have—which was even more valuable, was the empowering presence of God, the foundation of the Old Testament Scriptures, and the encouraging letters they received from Paul and others that later became part of the New Testament.

While millennia have passed since their time, and there are certain differences in what we face today, one thing will never change: God's faithfulness to protect and insulate us from evil is the foundation of peace and strength in our lives. It was the early believers' primary defense against the terror that Satan tried to spread among them every day. First Corinthians 2:16 says, "*We have the mind of Christ*" (various translations), and that mind strengthens us against the dark forces of evil. We exercise the mind of Christ within us by reading, studying, and applying God's Word to our lives and by listening to the voice of the Holy Spirit as He guides and directs us.

Remember, the God who lives within us is more real than anything in our physical world and greater than any dark spiritual forces that come against us. God's power not only counters our weaknesses but is somehow made perfect in them. Paul wrote, "[The Lord] *said to me, 'My grace is sufficient for you, for my power is made perfect in weakness'*" (2 Corinthians 12:9 NIV).

As born-again children of God, even though we live in a world filled with tests, trials, and troubles, we are citizens of heaven and heirs of God's promises. We belong to a kingdom filled with power, might, authority, protection, provision, preservation, and answers to dangers that intrude on our lives.

GOD'S FAITHFULNESS TO PROTECT AND INSULATE US FROM EVIL IS THE FOUNDATION OF PEACE AND STRENGTH IN OUR LIVES.

God's presence and Word build up our spiritual immune systems, making them inaccessible to demonic spirits that seek to infect our faith with all types of fear, including irrational fear. We are inoculated against ungodly anxiety as we apply God's truth and the blood of Jesus to our lives. Reading the Word is vital to us because it reminds us of the price Jesus paid to keep, protect, and shield us from all of the enemy's attacks.

Through His death on the cross, Christ not only took our diseases upon Himself, but He also paid the price for our peace: *"But he was pierced for our transgressions, he was crushed for our iniquities;* **the punishment that brought us peace was on him,** *and by his wounds we are healed"* (Isaiah 53:5 NIV). Jesus's precious blood frees and protects us: *"For you know that it was not with perishable things such as silver or gold that you were redeemed from the empty way of life handed down to you from your ancestors, but with the precious blood of Christ, a lamb without blemish or defect"* (1 Peter 1:18–19 NIV).

Again, people who do not have God's presence, power, Spirit, and Word in their lives are vulnerable to all kinds of evil; they are susceptible to being affected and infected by unauthorized spirits. But that does not need to be the case for the child of God. Never forget that Christ purchased your freedom from all forms of unnatural, ungodly fear by the nails that pierced His hands and feet, and by the crown of thorns the soldiers pressed on His brow. This includes freedom from the fear of sin, sickness, and death. In coming chapters, we will further explore the power of God's Word, the blood of Jesus, the name of Jesus, and prayer to conquer fear.

COUNTERING IRRATIONAL FEAR

Here are two essential ways to counteract irrational fear in your life: (1) govern your imagination and (2) cultivate your God-given creativity.

GOVERN YOUR IMAGINATION

Living a life free of fear requires governing our imaginations, not allowing our imaginations to control us. On that long-ago hunting trip in the forest, my overworked, colorful imagination awakened all the bear stories my uncles had told me when I was a child. My fears didn't need an actual bear to initiate a response of alarm, only an imagined bear. Our human imaginations are powerful enough to create wild stories, conjuring up scenarios that are not reality. We allow this to happen in many ways in our everyday lives as we work and interact with others, not just in an intensified situation such as I experienced.

Once more, the danger is that our imaginations can paralyze and divert us so that we forfeit some or all of what our present and future are meant to be. This is why we need to recognize that, in Christ, God has give us power, love, and a sound mind. When you sense fear being triggered by your imagination, I encourage you to take a step back, pray, read and reflect on God's Word, and seek the perspective of a trusted fellow believer. Govern your imagination according to biblical truths. If irrational fear has become a stronghold in your life, you may need to consult a qualified Christian counselor who can help walk you through the path to freedom.

CULTIVATE YOUR GOD-GIVEN CREATIVITY

As I learned from my experience with my high school friends, we should never allow the perspectives of others to project onto or incite in us their own irrational fears and insecurities. Because we live in a world infected with such unwarranted fears and insecurities, we must remain careful and prayerful in order to avoid becoming derailed by them. Instead, we must draw on our God-given courage and walk according to faith, despite what the world around us is saying and doing.

One of the ways we accomplish this is by cultivating a godly imagination that envisions and seeks what God can do in a given situation based on His Word, and by creating what is positive and uplifting to ourselves and others. Julia Cameron said, "Creativity is God's gift to us. Using our creativity is our gift back to God."[32] Genesis 1:26 explains that we carry the image of the Supreme Creator. He has endowed every person with creative gifts that reflect His own creativity. Exodus 35:31 says, *"And He has filled him with the Spirit of God, in wisdom, in understanding, in knowledge, and in all craftsmanship"* (NASB).

Remember that God created the world by merely speaking. Creative words inspired by God can change people and situations. Creativity flows like a river from the Holy Spirit, touching our hearts, inspiring our minds, and conveying visions of what is possible. Creativity activates God-given dreams, transforming them into reality. Creativity is the energy that helps bring purpose to our daily lives as we honor our connection to our Creator God.

Theologian Abraham Kuyper beautifully explains human creativity in this way: "The world of sounds, the world of forms, the world of tints, and the world of poetic ideas, can have no other source than God; and it is our privilege as bearers of His image, to have a perception of this beautiful world, artistically to reproduce, and humanly to enjoy it."[33] Our creativity reflects God's perfect creative character. The Lord has a purpose for each of us, whether our creative gifts involve words, artistic creations, business plans, ministry outreaches, problem-solving, or anything else.

I have heard people say to various artists, "You are so creative! I wish I were." The truth is that we all are creative, and to neglect our creative gifts—in the distinct way God has given them to us—is to contradict our design and purpose. It will even dishonor the Lord. And if we allow our gift of imagination to create false narratives, it will germinate fear and anger, which, as we have seen, will lead us down the wrong path for our lives.

God not only gave us the gift of imagination, but He gave it to us for good works! (See Ephesians 2:10.) Ask Him to help you to reject and remove any irrational fears that are blocking your path in life. Then you can build strong, healthy relationships with others, and God's Spirit will be able to flow through you, uninhibited, activating all the creative gifts He has given you so that the realm of God's kingdom on earth will flourish.

---

32. "Julia Cameron Quote," LibQuotes, https://libquotes.com/julia-cameron/quote/lbh9f2t.
33. Abraham Kuyper, *Calvinism: Six Stone Lectures*, reprint ed. (Apollo, PA: Ichthus Publications, 2020; New York: Fleming H. Revell, 1899), 138. Page number refers to the reprint edition.

7

FREEDOM FROM TRAUMA-BASED FEAR

"It has been well said that our anxiety does not empty to-morrow of its sorrows, but only empties to-day of its strength."
—*Charles Spurgeon*[34]

My earliest recollection of what fear feels like is of my being awakened from a deep sleep by angry voices, and then my mother threatening to take me away from my father forever. I was only four years old.

Although the incident occurred many years ago, the scene remains as clear in my mind as when it happened. It is still difficult for me to conceive how anyone so young could have been subjected to something so personally devastating. At the time, I experienced an emotional death in which my sense of innocence and security was suddenly ripped from me. Feelings of fear, panic, and terror—foreign to me up to that point—somehow sent my tiny soul back into a deep sleep for what may have been about fifteen minutes.

---

34. "Anxiety Does Not Empty Tomorrow of Its Sorrows; It Empties Today of Its Strength," Quote Investigator, https://quoteinvestigator.com/2021/07/03/anxiety/. Original quote attributed to Alexander McLaren.

Then, those two parental voices of frustration and anger, the ones that had just frightened my soul into a fetal position, suddenly broke through and awakened me again. It was almost as if they had summoned me out of the peaceful state in which I had been hiding, calling me back to the harsh reality of that waking nightmare.

I opened my eyes and cried, "Daddy? Momma? I think I just had a bad dream!"

Unfortunately, it wasn't just a bad dream. My mother, now using my cries for leverage against my father, pulled me close, looked directly into my eyes, and began to channel her frustration and anger through me, saying, "Don't worry, Son! We're going to live in New York—far, far away from here—where there's lots of snow."

But my little heart wasn't interested in going away to a place called New York or seeing the snow. Living in the Western United States, I didn't even know what snow was. I was in love with my home and the security of being with both my mother and father.

As soon as my mother finished her announcement, I began to beg her, "Please, Momma, please! No! I don't want you to leave Daddy. I don't want us to leave home!"

At that moment, my father broke down and began pleading with my mother for forgiveness for whatever he had done. "Please, honey, let's stop this! I love you! I know you love me, and we both love our children!"

To this day, I really don't know what happened to bring my mother and father to that place where they almost split up. My mother's anger may even have been justified. I don't know. But I do know this: I didn't deserve to go through an experience like that at such a young age, and neither does anyone else.

By some miracle, my father's words and emotional plea awakened my mother out of her anger, and the entire traumatic experience suddenly ended. Perhaps my mother recognized the softening that was occurring in my father's heart. The heated words, the anger, and the emotional turbulence all subsided. It was like a tornado that lost its energy and dissipated, ending its destructive path—but, tragically, not before leaving in its wake a strange mixture of calm and devastation in my heart.

The morning after the argument, I woke up with an odd sense of relief. Not because everything had suddenly become the way it used to be, but because my mother and father's relationship appeared to have been patched up, at least temporarily. Even so, my heart had been left with a gaping hole in it. While the fight between my parents may have lasted all of twenty-five minutes in their world, from my perspective as a four-year-old, it had seemed to last for hours. That traumatic event had injured my young soul. Not only that, but the incident was followed by years of additional family turmoil.

Although my parents were both born-again believers who loved God, their marriage was deeply troubled. What most people outside the family didn't know was that my mother, likely due to a combination of emotional and physical reasons, suffered from deep depression, extreme mood swings, and outbreaks of anger and rage. Holidays always seemed to be an especially stressful time, and the already strained celebrations frequently seemed to come to an abrupt end through some kind of argument or emotional explosion. My father, a gentle but strong man, struggled for years to hold the family together.

As I was growing up, this kind of turbulent life made me feel like I was trapped in a prison because I could not escape it. The fact that the outbursts and arguments, which seemed to come out of nowhere, could happen at any moment was terrifying to me. If it were not for God's intervention, I would have sustained damage to my mind, will, and emotions for the rest of my life.

In the months and years that followed that first traumatic incident, I wrestled with nightmares and an ungodly sense of fear that I would be left alone or abandoned. Even after I received Christ as my Savior and began a relationship with God, I continued to experience bouts of deep depression, insecurity, restlessness, chronic insomnia, and panic attacks. While I do have a number of fond family memories from my childhood when my mother and father seemed to be doing well, those moments always seemed to slip away or come to an abrupt halt by the occurrence of another emotional storm.

When I was about twelve years old, things appeared to be getting better. My mother and father began to work hard to resolve their issues, and they attended church regularly. By the time I was fifteen, it appeared as if things were indeed going well. My parents even began to serve in ministry, pastoring small churches in the area where we lived. Our family finally seemed to be on the road to normalcy.

But on my sixteenth birthday, all hell broke loose between my parents. It was as if we were all experiencing a reoccurring nightmare. This final disruption caused my brother and me to load up our clothes into a small, borrowed pickup truck and travel hundreds of miles away to stay with relatives. We believed we could begin a new life with them.

For a few short weeks, it felt like I had been given the fresh start I had hoped for. However, I quickly discovered that you can run away from a dysfunctional family or lifestyle and still take your baggage with you in the form of hidden scars. Struggling to process my confused emotions, I began to wander the streets. I battled deep depression and panic attacks and experienced bouts of frustration and anger. I was officially adrift— spiritually, emotionally, and physically.

Then, at the age of seventeen, I reached my lowest point. One evening, I found myself sitting on a dusty curb on a dimly lit side street in Bellflower, California, feeling as if I was at a completely dead end. Weeping from the depths of my being, I wondered if my life was worth living. For the first time I could recall, I began to question God. I remember thinking, "God, why would You allow me to be so alone like this? If You love me, why do I feel so afraid, so abandoned? God, where are You?"

As I sat and cried with my face buried in my hands, the air around me seemed to shift, and I felt a supernatural presence around me! When I removed my hands from my face and opened my eyes, I heard a voice I had discerned in my heart years earlier. It was the same comforting voice I had sensed when I was a small boy. The atmosphere around me felt infused with peace and power. I suddenly realized the voice I was hearing was the voice of the Holy Spirit speaking deep within my heart.

"Mark," He called, "you are not alone! I am right here with you. I have never left you, and I will never, ever leave you! Don't you see? I've been with you the entire time. I have come to remind you of My promise. I have given you My word that I will never leave or forsake you.… From this moment on, you will never doubt My presence!"

I felt love in a way I had never experienced before. My weeping turned into tears of joy. It was as if everything I had endured in my life now made sense. All my fear of the future lifted from me. It was as if someone had unlocked the door to my inner prison and freed me. The old feelings of fear, insecurity, and abandonment were removed and replaced with a hunger to free others from what I had been delivered from. In the same moment, I began to have what I can only describe as small visions of myself loving, helping, and ministering to people who had been wounded by similar experiences.

My encounter with the Holy Spirit that night ignited a chain reaction of life-changing events that transformed me and set me back on course toward fulfilling my God-given destiny. The encounter was so powerful that it changed the trajectory of my entire future.

As a result, I went back to the small town where I had been raised, made peace with my parents, and faced the powerful negative emotions that had almost destroyed me. In the subsequent months and years, God's call and anointing on my life were so strong that I started sharing my testimony with others. I joined a local worship team, singing and playing the piano for the group. Soon afterward, I assembled a band of musicians and singers, and I began to travel, sing, and share my testimony with everyone I met on the road. I shared my story in small settings, Christian nightclubs, church youth groups, and large gospel concerts across California and beyond.

MY ENCOUNTER WITH THE HOLY SPIRIT IGNITED A CHAIN REACTION OF LIFE-CHANGING EVENTS THAT TRANSFORMED ME AND SET ME BACK ON COURSE TOWARD FULFILLING MY GOD-GIVEN DESTINY.

Eventually, the Lord led me to the streets of San Francisco in the Tenderloin District, an area many people still consider to be one of the most dangerous in the city. There, my band was invited to participate in gospel music festivals, where we shared the good news of Jesus Christ in the main part of the district through music. As a result, hundreds of men and women—many of them prostitutes, drug dealers, drug addicts, and people oppressed or possessed by demons—were miraculously delivered by the power of God.

A few years later, I met and married the love of my life, and we were blessed with four amazing sons. Years later, I was invited to sing and share the gospel on some of the most prominent stages in the world, traveling to India, Africa, Europe, Israel, and South America. God blessed me to write and record several praise and worship songs. Some of those songs are still being shared around the world.

After years of global travel, I returned to the city where I had grown up and planted a church. There, Jordana and I have developed various ministry outreaches that help tens of thousands of people around the world to experience the same transforming power of the Holy Spirit that changed my life all those years ago. Today, in my sixties, I continue to sense that sweet, calming presence of the Holy Spirit that I experienced all those years ago.

THE HIDDEN EFFECTS OF TRAUMA

There is an important reason why I have shared intimate and painful details of my early life. Clearly, it is not to disgrace the memory of my dear mother and father. Thankfully, my parents also had a supernatural encounter with the Holy Spirit, finding healing and forgiveness in their marriage and personal relationships with God and with my older brother and me. Through the power of God, they became loving mates, caring parents, wonderful grandparents, and faithful members of our church before passing on to meet the Lord. Instead, I have shared my story to help people just like you identify and remove any unauthorized oppressive spirits that have come into your life due to trauma that you may be unwittingly carrying and fighting to overcome. I want to let you know that you are not alone.

Millions of people suffer from unnatural feelings of fear, frustration, and intense anxiety, and many of them cannot identify where those feelings originated. As I described earlier, I would have carried and entertained feelings of fear and abandonment for a lifetime if it had not been for the power of the Holy Spirit. The Spirit revealed to me where those feelings had come from and showed me how to face and defeat them. Otherwise, I would not be who I am or where I am today. Please understand that it is not because I have forgotten what I lived through but because God has freed me from its effects.

You might wonder how someone could forget a traumatic experience such as I described. The answer is that the human mind has the ability to file away painful experiences in the subconscious mind, where the brain secretly works to either solve them or hide them in order to protect us from further harm. Psychiatrist Judith Lewis Herman said, "After a traumatic experience, the human system of self-preservation seems to go onto permanent alert, as if the danger might return at any moment."[35]

The good news and the bad news is that your mind is more powerful than any supercomputer that exists on planet Earth. This means it has the capacity for far more than a one-track memory. When you have an experience, your brain, like a super-data recorder, captures everything about that moment and stores it in a compartment where it can be recalled. When I say "everything," I mean everything. Within moments of an event, all the details—such as words spoken, along with their perceived meaning; other sounds; tone; volume; sights; smells; tastes; touch; and anything else captured by the natural senses, intellect, and emotions is recorded and stored in our present consciousness and/or our subconscious mind.

Significantly, the word *subconscious* is composed of two elements. The prefix *sub-* comes from the idea of being or existing beneath or under something.[36] The term *conscious* can be defined as "aware of and responding to one's surroundings" and "having knowledge of something."[37] In essence, your subconscious is your "under-consciousness," which is made up of thousands of hidden awarenesses of incidents, as well as images from both negative and positive past experiences.

Traumatic events, like all other events, become captured and stored memories. These memories can be like a time bomb waiting to be ignited,

35. Rachel Sharpe, "100+ PTSD Quotes to Help Survivors Cope with Trauma," Declutter The Mind, February 27, 2021, https://declutterthemind.com/blog/ptsd-quotes/.
36. *Merriam-Webster.com Dictionary*, s.v. "sub," https://www.merriam-webster.com/dictionary/sub.
37. *Lexico*, s.v. "conscious," https://www.lexico.com/en/definition/conscious.

becoming potentially hazardous to our futures. The challenge is that painful feelings can resurface without warning, prompted by a resurrected memory or another form of reminder. That is the reason therapists and psychologists use terminology like "triggered" or "set off." The smallest test, challenge, or resistance can trigger fear at the very moment you need faith and courage.

It's possible to live your life secretly struggling with and/or suppressing fears that God has the power to deliver you from. If these latent toxic emotions from traumatic experiences are not identified and dealt with through the power of the Holy Spirit, they have the ability to derail your life or, worse, rob you of all that is essential to fulfilling your destiny.

People who fail to identify, confront, and eliminate hidden negative memories often experience what can be described as withdrawals, sudden collapses, or explosions. They suffer unnatural feelings of fear, anxiety, depression, anger, and frustration, and they may sometimes experience panic attacks. Again, these emotional collapses often occur when something or someone reconnects people to their painful memories.

When we are born again through Christ, our spirits (lowercase s) are reconciled or reconnected to God through the Holy Spirit (capital S), who locates, exposes, and transforms our painful memories into life-changing testimonies of victory over fear. He also gives us spiritual weapons to combat the powers of darkness that would seek to enter or reenter our lives. Isaiah 61:3 presents us with these astonishing and calming words:

> *To console those who mourn in Zion, to give them beauty for ashes, the oil of joy for mourning, the garment of praise for the spirit of heaviness; that they may be called trees of righteousness, the planting of the LORD, that He may be glorified.*　　　　　　　　　　　　　　　　(NKJV)

The *English Standard Version*'s translation of this verse paints perhaps an even more profound picture for us of God's healing power: "*To grant to those who mourn in Zion—to give them a beautiful headdress instead of ashes, the oil of gladness instead of mourning, the garment of praise instead of a faint spirit; that they may be called oaks of righteousness, the planting of the Lord, that he may be glorified.*"

"To give them a beautiful headdress instead of ashes"—this denotes exchanging the leftovers of a tragic, broken life for the supernatural peace, joy, and covering provided by God for the minds and hearts of His children. This is precisely what God does! He replaces our sadness with joy, our panic with peace, our mourning with laughter, and our weakness with power. He grants us supernatural faith and courage in the face of adversity.

GOD REPLACES OUR SADNESS WITH JOY, OUR PANIC WITH PEACE, OUR MOURNING WITH LAUGHTER, AND OUR WEAKNESS WITH POWER.

TRACK YOUR FEARS

One of the first steps to healing is to try to identify the origins of your fears. If you were to track your ungodly fears backward in time, where would they lead you? Where did those feelings originate? As I learned in my situation, demon-induced anxiety or irrational fears may sometimes be traced to a particular traumatic experience where they were first conceived. Demonic spirits use unaddressed traumatic experiences as a way of gaining access to our thought life, and then they use our thoughts to torment us. This is especially true of those negative experiences that we hide or, worse, refuse to identify because we are fearful of facing and addressing them.

To be clear, not all fears and panic attacks can be attributed to a human cause. Some can clearly be traced back to some form of demonic attack. However, God enables us to resist and expel the oppressive spirits that continue to assault us through our painful memories and anxiety. Believers have been deputized by the Lord to expunge evil spirits from their own lives by the power of the Holy Spirit.

In the New Testament, there are many examples of people being delivered from demons by God's power. Jesus cast out evil spirits multiple times. (See, for example, Matthew 8:16.) The circumstances are described in detail several times. Jesus cast out demons from a man who was mute (see Matthew 9:32–33; Luke 11:14), a man in a synagogue (see Mark 1:21–28;

Luke 4:31–37), and from men living among the tombs in the region of the Gadarenes or Gerasenes (see Matthew 8:28–34; Mark 5:1–17). Jesus also cast out demons from a little girl (see Matthew 15:21–28) and from a young boy (Matthew 17:14–20).

Furthermore, Jesus gave His disciples the authority to cast out demons. The seventy-two disciples He commissioned to go out and proclaim the good news of the kingdom returned from their mission with joy, saying, *"Lord, even the demons submit to us in your name"* (Luke 10:17 NIV). After the outpouring of the Holy Spirit at Pentecost, Jesus's followers continued to cast out demons. (See, for example, Acts 5:16; 8:7.) The apostle Paul cast out a spirit of divination from a servant girl. (See Acts 16:16–18.)

I want to clarify that I'm not suggesting born-again, Spirit-filled believers can be demon-possessed. I am saying that God's Word teaches us we have authority through the indwelling Holy Spirit to identify evil spirits that are oppressing us and others, and to stop them in their tracks. While demons carry no authority to possess believers because the blood of Jesus paid for our protection, they will do everything in their power to trouble us! This is why it is so important for us to identify areas of our lives where we have experienced trauma and to turn all those areas over to the Holy Spirit so He can heal us and give us His peace. By doing so, we reduce the risk of allowing demonic powers to use our negative experiences to oppress us.

It is interesting that the noun oppression, which is defined as "unjust or cruel exercise of authority or power," comes from a Latin word meaning "action of pressing on or overpowering."[38] The verb oppress means "to crush or burden by abuse of power or authority" and "to burden spiritually or mentally : weigh heavily upon."

I wonder how many born-again, Spirit-filled believers, while not demonically possessed, suffer because they are demonically oppressed? Thankfully, the Holy Spirit has given us every tool we need to become free—and stay free.

---

38. *Merriam-Webster.com Dictionary*, s.v. "oppression," https://www.merriam-webster.com/dictionary/oppression.

BRING YOUR FEARS TO THE LORD

Sadly, multitudes of people, including Christians, ignore their symptoms of trauma and simply learn to accept their unnatural fears as a way of life without ever daring to identify and confront them. If a memory of a traumatic experience from your life has suddenly surfaced while you have been reading this chapter, that is actually an indication that you're making headway and recapturing lost spiritual territory. Or, perhaps you were already aware of the trauma in your life but haven't been able to overcome its effects. Together, let's keep moving forward, never backward, so you can be set free. *"So then, just as you received Christ Jesus as Lord, continue to live your lives in him, rooted and built up in him, strengthened in the faith as you were taught, and overflowing with thankfulness"* (Colossians 2:6–7 NIV).

Read the following words carefully: *You no longer have to accept a life in which you struggle with ungodly fear and anxiety.* As a child of God, you can be set free. God can and will deliver you, just as He delivered me. Micah Christopher's song "No More Fear" is like an anthem to God for saving and delivering us. Here are two lines from that song:

You are the peace in the night

You turn the darkness into light[39]

To receive your healing, you don't have to completely reinvent the wheel. I believe you were drawn to this book for a specific reason. Maybe its title reached out to you and whispered, "I can help you!" God uses people like me to share stories and principles of deliverance drawn from years of experience and accumulated wisdom. We become models for others so they can leave behind their wildernesses and move toward their God-ordained successes. No matter your condition of fear, you do not have to live with it. You can begin to do something about it right now.

All of us, if we are wise, can glean much from those who lived before us, as well as from other people today who have gone through experiences similar to the ones we have gone through or are going through. The truths and principles in the Bible, accounts from history, and the men and women called by God to teach and counsel us can help us to avoid mistakes we

39. "'No More Fear' Lyrics," New Release Today, https://www.newreleasetoday.com/lyricsdetail.php?lyrics_id=113637.

would have made and wrong paths we would have taken if God had not directed us to those resources. They help to cut years off our learning curves and move us along the path to freedom much faster than we could have traveled on our own. I pray that *Fear Must Not Win* is, even now, one of those helpful resources for you.

This chapter is not about dealing with the psychology of the mind, although the insights of psychology can be helpful for defining the issues involved. Again, the real answer to receiving healing is to experience the supernatural, victorious power of God. The Spirit of God exposes the enemy's carefully crafted plans and gives us the weapons of spiritual warfare to weaken and destroy those plans. The creative power of God's presence and Word will awaken the champion within you and remove your fear so that you can discover the faith God has placed within you and courageously slay every giant that dares to stand against you and your God-given destiny.

> **YOU NO LONGER HAVE TO ACCEPT A LIFE IN WHICH YOU STRUGGLE WITH UNGODLY FEAR AND ANXIETY. AS A CHILD OF GOD, YOU CAN BE SET FREE.**

FEAR HAS A WEAKNESS

When God was healing me of trauma-based fear, He showed me a major secret to receiving healing: fear has a weakness! When we target fear's vulnerability, it will flee from us. The power that overcomes fear is like a light that dispels darkness (or even like kryptonite that saps the power of the fictional character Superman). It is a power that we have been talking about throughout this book, and which we will discuss more fully in coming chapters: the creative power of God's presence and Word, as well as the force of our God-given faith. These elements are so potent that they send fear running for cover!

I remember the day when I realized I didn't have to be a slave to fear one moment longer. It began when I opened my Bible and started reading aloud, and something shifted within me. I could feel the atmosphere in my life change, as if someone had lifted a shade or pulled back a curtain and let the sunshine in. I could also describe this experience as a form of detox; I was being cleansed of tormenting, fearful thoughts, which were now being drained from the pores of my soul.

What made the difference was that I began to take hold of truths and promises from God's Word and apply them to myself personally. When I made these declarations of faith, my soul felt lighter and lighter, as if weights were being lifted off my heart and mind.

Finally, it hit me: I was experiencing what the psalmist described when he prayed, *"Your word is a lamp to my feet, and a light to my path"* (Psalm 119:105 KJVER). I had been living without fully applying the incredible superpower of God's Word to my personal situation. That had been like trying to find my way in the pitch darkness in an unfamiliar area or working to repair something without having the proper tools. No wonder it is so hard for many people to see beyond their pain or escape their ungodly fears!

I thought back to the times when the fears I carried had almost overwhelmed me, leaving me little hope for my future. Suddenly, I realized that *where there was no Word, there was no light to see my future.* And having no light gives fear a place to hide. But now, as I received God's Word, it was like going from using a dimly lit candle to travel on a dark, rough path to using the high beams of a large vehicle on a clear night to drive on a major freeway.

Not only did I begin to catch glimpses of my good future in God, but the words I was reading also started to expose every trick the enemy had been playing on me all those years. It was almost too much to wrap my mind around. God's power had been within my reach the entire time. How could I have allowed the devil, that diabolical thief, to steal so many years of my life, not to mention my sense of peace, joy, and security?

The morning after I had this revelation, I woke up feeling different inside. Previously, I had always woken up with a cold feeling in my stomach. Now, all of my soul's aches and pains seemed to be gone. That evening, after work, I could hardly wait to read more of the Word. I opened my Bible, and chills ran up my spine as I read these words:

When I am afraid, I will put my trust in You. In God, whose word
I praise, in God I have put my trust; I shall not be afraid. What can
mere mortals do to me? (Psalm 56:3–4 NASB)

Just as I was about to turn to the next page, I heard the Holy Spirit say, in my heart, "Pray this!" So, I did. "Father, in Jesus's name, I pray, '*When I am afraid, I will put my trust in You. In* [You], *whose word I praise, in* [You] *I have put my trust; I shall* **not** *be afraid. What can mere mortals do to me?*'" I searched the Scriptures for another passage about winning victory over fear, and I came across the portion of the book of Isaiah where the prophet declared this word from the Lord: "*So do not fear, for I am with you; do not be dismayed, for I am your God. I will strengthen you and help you; I will uphold you with my righteous right hand*" (Isaiah 41:10 NIV).

That night, I determined in my heart that I would never live in fear another day of my life. If I were going to be entirely delivered from ungodly fears, anxiety, and panic attacks, I would have to make reading and applying God's promises my lifestyle. And that is what I did. Over the course of the next year, I felt stronger and stronger until, finally, it hit me like a ton of bricks: Where was the fear? Where was my oppressor? I was no longer suffering a single attack!

Months and then years passed until, finally, I had an epiphany. I was preparing to be picked up and transported to where I was scheduled to speak, and I began to laugh out loud as joy flooded my spirit. After years of believing I would have to suffer forever from ungodly anxiety and panic attacks, I was now continually walking and resting in God's Word, will, and presence. The devil had fled!

It was as if the shoe was on the other foot. Whereas, all those years earlier, I had found myself hiding from fear, now fear itself seemed to be in panic mode, desperate to get away, because I was sharing with others what God had done to release me. I had discovered this powerful spiritual truth: the more space I granted to God's Word in my life, the less space fear found to hide. Fear had given way to victory. Weakness could no longer occupy the same space as strength. A newfound, courageous, faith-infused vision for the future began to course through my spiritual veins.

No matter what fears you are facing, I believe that you, too, can be delivered as you put into practice the biblical principles in this chapter and the rest of this book. It will likely be a process, as it was for me, even though I also had a profound supernatural healing of my emotions when I was seventeen that transformed my life. Let me assure you: the Holy Spirit wants to minister to you to release you from deep emotional pain. As I mentioned in the previous chapter, along the way, you may need the assistance of a qualified counselor to help you find healing from your trauma. You can also ask trusted brothers and sisters in Christ to pray on your behalf as you read the Word and stand in faith. The Holy Spirit will continue to work in your life to heal you of your painful memories. And then, you will suddenly ask, as I did, "Where is the fear?" because you will have set fear on the run, defeating the oppressor!

8

OVERCOMING ENTRENCHED FEARS AND INSURMOUNTABLE ODDS

> "Every person who has grown to any degree of usefulness, every person who has grown to distinction, almost without exception has been a person who has risen by overcoming obstacles, by removing difficulties, by resolving that when he met discouragement he would not give up."
> —*Booker T. Washington*[40]

Over the years, Jordana and I have had the honor of meeting some fascinating men and women from the United States and around the world, but we would place Desiree and Mel Ayres near the top of our list. What makes this couple unique is not the fact that they pastor one of the fastest-growing ministries in the Hollywood, California, area, but that they both once worked in the entertainment industry, and they are now dedicated to sharing Jesus with the Hollywood community and beyond.

If ever the old adage "You can't judge a book by its cover" applied to anyone, it certainly applies to my friends Desiree and Mel. Both are

---

40. "Booker T. Washington Quote," LibQuotes, https://libquotes.com/booker-t-washington/quote/lbj8y1j.

anointed communicators, soulwinners, and planet-shakers for God. Apart from reading this chapter of the book, if you met them, you probably never would have imagined some of the things they have experienced and gone through.

For example, you might not have guessed that Mel was an aspiring actor who appeared in some of Hollywood's most popular daytime television series, such as *Days of Our Lives* and *Falcon Crest*. Or that when Mel gave his heart to the Lord, he left all Hollywood had to offer him in order to follow Jesus Christ and share the gospel with the lost and dying. I have to say, he's gifted at it! When I am with Mel, he is almost always witnessing to someone and leading them to the Lord. His heart for people is a clear reflection of the heavenly Father's heart.

But what makes my friend Mel even more interesting is that he happens to be married to Batman's daughter. No, not the "real" Batman, but the one you may have watched take all those physical kicks and punches on the 1960s hit TV series. You see, Desiree's father, Hubie Kerns, was one of the most influential stunt coordinators in Hollywood, and he was the stunt double for Adam West, the actor who played the title character of Batman. Desiree's mother, Doris Mae Kerns, was actress Elizabeth Taylor's personal publicist and best friend for years.

Desiree's story, which she relates in this chapter, is fascinating not because of her parents' relationship with the influential world of the Hollywood film industry or the fact that she decided to follow her famous father into the stunt business. It is because she struggled with a deeply entrenched fear and then faced what appeared to be insurmountable odds of survival after one of her Hollywood stunts almost took her life. Even more profound is the way in which God delivered her from fear and miraculously healed her by the creative power of His presence and Word.

There may be times when we, too, find ourselves facing an entrenched fear or a seemingly insurmountable circumstance that threatens an area of our lives or even our physical existence. That area may be our health, our finances, a family relationship, or our God-given vision. Such overwhelming circumstances can become a tremendous source of fear if we haven't fortified ourselves against anxiety and panic ahead of time—or if we don't learn to contend with our fear as we go through the trial.

How do we face such overpowering obstacles without giving in to fear? There are several specific principles that will help us to triumph over forces that would otherwise overwhelm us. I wanted to share Desiree's story as a tremendous illustration of what it means to practice these principles and have them in your spiritual arsenal when they are needed the most.

A FATHER'S EXAMPLE

Desiree credits her ability to overcome her fear to her heavenly Father and to the lessons her earthly father taught her.

"I loved my dad with all my heart," she says. "He was my hero, and I learned so much from him. In fact, little did I know that something he taught me would later become the very thing that would deliver me from the spirit of fear and save my life in a crisis.

"Besides my husband, my dad was one of the greatest men I've ever known. While the Lord used Mel to lead me to Christ, it was my father who witnessed to me day and night. My dad was the one who introduced me to the power of the Holy Spirit.

"When I was young, I wasn't interested in anything to do with Christianity. I didn't know it at the time, but my father was praying with some of his close friends that I would get saved and meet a good Christian man. His prayers worked! I met Mel, and we were married a few short months later.

"I fell head over heels in love with Mel the minute I laid eyes on him! But the thing that blew me away about him was that he carried his Bible everywhere. I knew there was something special about him. I now believe that something special was his love for God and the anointing on his life."

AN ENTRENCHED FEAR

Even though Desiree was happily married, she had a deeply rooted obstacle of fear in her life.

"By the time of our marriage, I had already begun to follow in my father's footsteps and work with him in the stunt business. I loved my job because it required me to do everything I already enjoyed doing. I felt like the luckiest girl in the world. After all, I got up every day, went to a film set somewhere in the world, and got paid to have fun!

"I guess I take after my father because I am a bit of an adrenaline junky. I love to jet ski, snow ski, deep dive, all of it. But there was one thing I absolutely hated more than anything; I mean, I despised it: *I hated heights*. I was scared to death of them! While I may have appeared fearless, before I received Christ and got God's Word inside of me, I could not stand high places of any kind.

"However, as I started to get more and more into the stunt business, my father began to talk to me about taking on some of the riskier stunt work. 'Desiree,' he said, 'the real money is in doing jumps and fire stunts.' What's funny is that my father knew I hated heights. Think about it: who wants to be thrown up into the air, fall from tall buildings, or be set on fire? But I tried the fire stunts, and once I got used to suiting up and putting on fire-protective gel and gear, doing those stunts was really no big deal!

"Ironically, while this was something I learned to master, it would be the very thing that would come to try to take my life a few short months later. I'm not just talking about fire; I'm talking about the spirit of fear itself. And while I learned how to do the fire stunts from my father, the truth is, I was still deathly afraid of heights."

Desiree Ayres was a stunt woman who hated heights! Knowing her story, this aspect is especially significant because, in a spiritual sense, that was exactly where God would train her to go—to the high places to fight for her life and for God's kingdom. The circumstances she faced remind me of Ephesians 6:12: "*For we do not wrestle against flesh and blood, but against the rulers, against the authorities, against the cosmic powers over this present darkness, against the spiritual forces of evil in the heavenly places*" (ESV).

God wants to make us, His beloved children, fearless! Why? He's training us for the future, specifically, to live and battle in the high places. This not only means waging war for the kingdom through spiritual warfare but also first being established in our true position in Christ: "*And God raised us up with Christ and seated us with him in the heavenly realms in Christ Jesus*" (Ephesians 2:6 NIV). Only when we learn how to live from that place of authority where Christ is seated in the heavenly realms can we defeat the enemy's schemes to incapacitate us with fear.

GOING TO THE HIGH PLACES

Desiree explains how she began her journey to the "high places."

"When I finally told my father I didn't want to do anything that required jumping off high places or leaping from tall buildings," she says, "he did something that, at the time, he didn't know would later save my life.

"'I know exactly how to teach you how to overcome your fear of high places!' he said.

"'You know I hate heights!' I exclaimed.

"I wasn't sure what my dad was thinking, but, for me, jumping from a high place, even if it was with cables, wasn't a good idea for someone who was terrorized by the thought of just being five feet off the ground. But I thought, 'If I can't trust my father, who can I trust?'

"What I didn't know was that my father was up to something more than teaching me how to overcome my fear of heights. He was about to introduce me to the creative power of God's presence and His Word. His plan not only taught me to face my fear of heights but also to face the demonic spirit of fear that I would later have to meet head-on.

"My father was smart. He started me off very small. He didn't begin by teaching me how to jump from high places. He had me jump off a step ladder only a few feet at a time. As he taught me to jump, he also taught me to rely on the Word of God, which would empower me to overcome all my fears."

Just as Desiree's father took her out of her comfort zone so she could learn not to be afraid of heights, God often allows us to face what feels like dangerous territory to train us not to fear the people and circumstances that are making us afraid. He does this not just to teach us how to face specific tests or trials, but also to show us how to face any type of fear—whether irrational fear, trauma-based fear, or something else—along with the demonic spirit of fear itself.

GOD OFTEN ALLOWS US TO FACE WHAT FEELS LIKE DANGEROUS TERRITORY TO TRAIN US NOT TO FEAR THE PEOPLE AND CIRCUMSTANCES THAT ARE MAKING US AFRAID.

REPEATING AND INTERNALIZING GOD'S WORD

Desiree describes what enabled her to defeat her entrenched fear of heights step-by-step.

"To help me overcome my fear of heights, my dad taught me how to quote the Word of God *before each and every jump, on every level.* I believe he started me out at about only two feet. Each time, he would have me quote 2 Timothy 1:7 until I felt confident enough to jump from a higher level. 'Desiree,' he said, 'I now want you to memorize this verse. I want you to learn to repeat it again and again. Say it until you feel the courage to leap, then jump! Come on, let's say it together: *"God has not given us the spirit of fear; but of power, and of love, and of a sound mind"'* [2 Timothy 1:7 KJVER].

"Before I knew it, I was performing stunts from as high as thirty feet, and as high as two hundred and fifty feet with cables. This is something I never would have done before my dad infused the Word of God into my spirit."

We often underestimate the powerful impact that reading, meditating on, and declaring the Word of God can have in our lives for overcoming fear. In the previous chapter, I shared about my struggles with fear due to childhood trauma. I explained that what made a vast difference in my life was when I began to take hold of truths and promises from God's Word *and apply them to myself personally.* (In chapter 10, we will talk further about what it means to follow God's instructions through His Word and Spirit.)

The following passage from Deuteronomy explains how we should fill our lives and hearts with God's Word:

These words, which I am commanding you today, shall be [written] on your heart and mind. You shall teach them diligently to your children [impressing God's precepts on their minds and penetrating their hearts with His truths] and shall speak of them when you sit in your house and when you walk on the road and when you lie down and when you get up. And you shall bind them as a sign on your hand (forearm), and they shall be used as bands (frontals, frontlets) on your forehead. You shall write them on the doorposts of your house and on your gates.

(Deuteronomy 6:6–9 AMP)

Desiree further explains the impact that declaring God's Word had on her life. "My father would say, 'Des, I want you to practice saying 2 Timothy 1:7 out loud as many times as you need to before every jump.' To my amazement, every time I quoted those words, fear seemed to just leave my body as if it was melting off me. I learned to quote that verse before I performed every stunt. Within a few months, I was jumping and doing major stunts like a pro, just as my father had taught me to.

"As a result, I found myself working on major television programs and films like *Miami Vice; Knight Rider; The Fall Guy; Murder, She Wrote; Matt Houston; History of the World; 1941*; and many others. It was all risky work, but that was my job as a stunt woman, and I enjoyed it."

THE FIRE OF ADVERSITY

Desiree's declaration of God's Word prepared her for the biggest challenge of her life.

"Things were going extremely well for Mel and me until, one day, I received an invitation to work on a major television series called *Airwolf*. While I was excited about the opportunity to work on the set of one of the most popular television programs at that time, something just didn't feel right about it. To be completely honest, in retrospect, I think the Lord was warning me. But because it was such a hit show, I knew the money would be good, and I took the job.

"As the day of my stunt neared, I thought to myself, 'How hard can it be?' I had performed similar stunts many times before. This stunt called for me to drive a jeep and push a button that would open the hood and set off a simple smoke bomb to give the appearance of an explosion. When I pressed the button, I would be ejected free and clear from the vehicle, roll out, dust myself off, and go home. I presupposed, 'Job well done, right?'

"When we rehearsed the stunt, everything went just as planned. But on the day we were scheduled to film the actual stunt, something went horribly wrong. Instead of loading a harmless smoke bomb into the jeep I was to drive, someone on the crew mistakenly loaded a fourteen-pound naphthalene bomb. Naphthalene is a highly explosive material.

"I got into the vehicle, and, after hearing the director shout, 'Action!' I took off. When I reached my stunt execution point, I hit the button to open the hood of the jeep, set off the smoke bomb, and be ejected out of the vehicle clear of harm. Unfortunately—or perhaps fortunately—that is the last thing I remember about that stunt.

"When I pressed the button, it ignited that fourteen-pound naphthalene bomb, launching me high into the air and setting me on fire, causing me great bodily harm. Of course, the explosion knocked me unconscious. When I came to, I discovered I had been seriously burned. The next thing I knew, I was being airlifted to the nearest hospital, where I was admitted into the intensive care unit. It was there that I would discover just how bad things really were."

A DETERMINED FAITH

Desiree continues, "I was in horrific pain from my burns and injuries. On top of that, when the doctors gave me morphine, I had a severe allergic reaction to the medication that could have taken my life, as well, had it not been for the grace of God.

"My father came to see me as soon as he received the news. When he walked into my room and saw the condition I was in, he began to cry. He was devastated. I think he felt responsible for getting me into the stunt business. Within minutes, Mel arrived too. Mel really isn't a super-emotional, crying kind of guy. But when he walked in and saw me, he broke down in tears. Because he didn't want to upset me, he worked hard to hide his emotions.

"Finally, the doctors came in and gave us their report. I had cuts, scrapes, bruises, and, worst of all, severe burns on my neck and face. My upper lip had practically been burned off. Because the jeep was supposed to be carrying just a smoke bomb, I hadn't been wearing any kind of fire-protective gear, gel, or even a face mask. The only thing that saved my hair was that I had been wearing a wig. Otherwise, it would have been even worse.

"The pain was terrible. All I could do was pray and quote the Scriptures. We decided to stand on the promise of Proverbs 4:20–23, which says, 'Be *attentive to my words; incline your ear to my sayings. Let them not escape from your sight; keep them within your heart. For they are life to those who find them, and healing to all their flesh. Keep your heart with all vigilance, for from it flow the springs of life'* [ESV]."

In the years and months leading up to everything Desiree now faced, her father had taught her not only to overcome her fears but also to battle the powers of darkness that had come to take her life. She fought this battle by repeating God's Word over and over again and experiencing its creative power to protect, heal, and bring peace. She explains how she responded to her fear during this time.

"Any time fear tried to come to me, I just started quoting the passage my father had taught me to memorize, 2 Timothy 1:7: '*God has not given us the spirit of fear; but of power, and of love, and of a sound mind'* [KJVER]. All I had now was the God my father had introduced me to and my husband had led me to receive! I knew that no one but God had the power to heal and restore me.

"I remember getting a phone call from one of the other stunt gals who was working on set. When I answered the phone, she immediately began to cry and express sympathy. While I know she was trying to comfort me, I just dropped the phone! I didn't need or want anyone speaking or acting like I was going to be in that condition for the rest of my life. I didn't want people crying over me. I needed people who had *faith*. I was believing for my healing, and there was no turning back!

"That day, I asked Mel to go find every teaching tape on faith we had and bring it to me. He brought me teachings by Kenneth Copeland, Kenneth Hagin, and Fred Price, and every praise and worship tape or CD we had. Over the following days, I did nothing but pray and listen to teachings on faith, divine healing, miracles, and deliverance.

"I am so grateful for Mel. He would come to see me every day and encourage me. His faith never wavered. He would say, 'Des, God is going to completely heal you. And when He does, you will be even more beautiful than you were when I first met you!'"

DESIREE FOUGHT HER BATTLE AGAINST THE POWERS OF DARKNESS BY REPEATING GOD'S WORD OVER AND OVER AGAIN AND EXPERIENCING ITS CREATIVE POWER TO PROTECT, HEAL, AND BRING PEACE.

THE POWER OF WORSHIP AND THE WORD

As Desiree stood in faith and declared God's Word, the doctors were amazed at her rapid improvement.

"Ten days later," she says, "I walked out of that hospital, something no one thought I would be able to do. But while I was on the mend overall, my face and neck were still covered in bandages. I needed a creative miracle! While I knew God was healing me and doing a work in my body, I continued to be in terrible pain because some of the dirt and gravel was still in the skin of my neck and in my upper lip.

"The enemy tried to make me afraid and discourage me, but I refused to listen to him. Instead of crying, feeling sorry for myself, or complaining, I began to praise and worship God. For hours, I would quote the Scripture my dad had taught me and worship God, bandages and all!

"Finally, one day, I was in such pain that I could hardly bear it. At that point, I was so sick of wearing those bandages. I remember the devil trying to tell me, 'Desiree, you will never be healed. You will never look the same!' I decided I was going to take a shower, and when I turned on the water, I could feel it hitting the bandages and my wounds, and it hurt so badly. But I began to cry out to the Lord. I praised God, quoting the Word with every bit of faith I could muster. I stood under the shower worshipping until I was lost in the Spirit.

"After a few minutes, something supernatural happened! As I was worshipping God, I felt the Holy Spirit fill every square inch of the shower space I was standing in. Within a moment's time, I felt an unexplainable calm come over me. When I turned off the water and looked down, I saw that all my bandages were lying on the shower floor. When I looked closer, I noticed that they weren't in a pile. They were all neatly folded up, resting at my feet! And I was fully healed! I began to cry and praise God.

"There is so much more I could say about what God did for me, but it would take me all day to tell you about God's goodness!"[41]

PRINCIPLES FOR OVERCOMING

The principles for overcoming entrenched fear and insurmountable odds demonstrated by Desiree's story have entered my heart and mind and become revelation that has ignited something deep within my spirit. I believe the Lord wants to ignite them within your spirit too. We have discussed some of these principles in other contexts in previous chapters, and we will explore others in the rest of this book. I encourage you to read and reflect on the following points until they become so deeply embedded in your spirit that hell itself won't be able to steal them from you, no matter what you may face in life.

1. *Trust completely in God.* Although Desiree had an entrenched fear of heights, she trusted her father's plan to help her overcome her fear, and she followed his instructions even though she was uncertain about them. She started with small jumps and moved on to larger and larger ones until her fear melted away. In the same way, we can trust our heavenly Father's plan to bring us step-by-step into a fear-free life and the purposes He has for us. It just takes trusting in His wisdom and practicing obedience to His Word one truth at a time.

2. *Saturate yourself with God's Word.* Desiree discovered the creative power of God's presence and Word to heal and deliver. Her father's plan to free her from fear not only taught her to face her particular fear of heights, but it also showed her how to face the demonic spirit of fear that she would

41. Used by permission of Desiree Ayres. Desiree tells her story in full in her book *Beyond the Flame: A Journey from Burning Devastation to Healing Restoration* (Lake Mary, FL: Creation House, 2012).

need to fight against after her accident. Moreover, the Word that she received into her heart empowered her to be able to win battles against fear for the rest of her life.

Don't wait until you experience a trial or are faced with what appears to be an insurmountable problem before you fill your heart with God's Word. Prepare for difficult times right now. Jesus said, *"I have told you these things, so that in me you may have peace. In this world you will have trouble. But take heart! I have overcome the world"* (John 16:33 NIV). Learn to quote Scripture to yourself as you encounter challenges and obstacles throughout your day, just as Desiree quoted Scripture before each of her jumps.

3. *Train for the high places.* When we go through specific tests, trials, or negative experiences, we are not only learning to face our natural fears and the spirit of fear itself but to live a fear-free lifestyle. The Lord is teaching us to reign in Him so we can cast down principalities and powers from the realm of darkness. We are being trained as spiritual warriors to bring God's kingdom to earth.

4. *When you are in pain—physically or emotionally—continually pray and quote the Scriptures.* No matter how difficult things seem, keep filling your mind and heart with God's Word. As Desiree did, decide right now to stand on Proverbs 4:20–23: *"Be attentive to my words; incline your ear to my sayings. Let them not escape from your sight; keep them within your heart. For they are life to those who find them, and healing to all their flesh. Keep your heart with all vigilance, for from it flow the springs of life"* (ESV).

NO MATTER HOW DIFFICULT THINGS SEEM, KEEP FILLING YOUR MIND AND HEART WITH GOD'S WORD.

---

5. *Stand in faith.* Recognize that even well-intentioned sympathy will not bring about deliverance and healing. We need to exercise faith that God is with us and is working out His purposes in our lives. He will set us free. Refuse to listen to anyone or anything that would initiate or perpetuate fear and a lack of faith and courage. Read and listen to teachings

on the subject of faith and miracles. Keep company with people who will spiritually lift you up, strengthening your faith.

6. *Praise and worship God.* Instead of feeling sorry for yourself and complaining, praise and worship God. Desiree said she praised and worshipped God and quoted His Word for hours. And it was when she was praising and worshipping God that she was healed and her bandages fell off. Similarly, as you worship God, rest in the presence of the Holy Spirit. Allow Him to remove the mental and emotional bandages that have concealed your painful wounds. Then let Him fill your heart and spirit as He does His healing work in your life.

HELP FROM THE LORD

Perhaps you're in a place where you feel like you are walking through the valley of the shadow of death. I believe this chapter of the book is for you. The Lord loves you so much and wants you to be set free from fear, wounds, pain, and bondage. Millions of men and women are needlessly suffering because no one has ever talked with them about how to be free from fear and oppression. Perhaps you are struggling with an entrenched fear or are facing a seemingly insurmountable situation. You may even be in a hospital bed like Desiree was. You may be laboring to find the courage to face another day. If you are in any of these situations, there's more than hope for you, there is *help*—help from the Lord.

I believe God wants you to have a divine encounter to bring you through your situation. He wants to deliver you from fear and teach you how to live in heavenly places with Christ so you can engage in spiritual battles in the high places! Just as Desiree's father taught her how to overcome her fear, your heavenly Father wants you to reach new levels of fearless living. You can live a bold and courageous life. In the most difficult of circumstances, God desires to reveal Himself to you and restore you from the inside out.

PART THREE

PRINCIPLES FOR FEAR-FREE LIVING

9

GOD'S MANIFEST PRESENCE

"We may ignore, but we can nowhere evade,
the presence of God. The world is crowded with Him.
He walks everywhere incognito."
—*C. S. Lewis*[42]

We will now take a closer look at some key biblical principles for becoming free of fear, beginning with our lifeline—the presence of God. True peace, protection, and prosperity come from being in God's presence. His presence in our hearts provides the strength, hope, and confidence we need to overcome all our anxiety and trepidation. François Fénelon, the renowned Christian mystic, said, "The presence of God calms the soul, and gives it quiet and repose."[43]

This is why we must be mindful of God's presence in our lives every moment of the day. It's one thing to understand that God is real, but it is another thing to truly know that He is with us. We need to move from a mere acknowledgment of His existence to an ongoing experience of and

---

42. Quotes of Famous People, https://quotepark.com/quotes/2101896-clive-staples-lewis-we-may-ignore-but-we-can-nowhere-evade-the-prese/.
43. "François Fénelon Quote," LibQuotes, https://libquotes.com/fran%C3%A7ois-f%C3%A9nelon/quote/lbx2b1d.

reliance on Him, even when we do not tangibly sense that He is near. As Scottish minister Robert Murray McCheyne said, "If I could hear Christ praying for me in the next room, I would not fear a million of enemies. Yet distance makes no difference; He is praying for me."[44]

GOD DESIRES TO BE WITH HIS PEOPLE

We must first understand that God not only created human beings, but, from the start, He has desired to be near us, to share His love with us, to fellowship with us, to be one with us. The Lord was with Adam and Eve in the garden of Eden; He would walk with them in *"the cool of the day"* (Genesis 3:8 NIV). He was with the Hebrews when He rescued them from slavery in Egypt, manifesting His presence in a pillar of cloud by day and a pillar of fire by night. (See, for example, Exodus 13:21–22.) In the Israelites' tabernacle, and later the temple, the specific focal point of God's presence was the ark of the covenant in the holy of holies. God told Moses, *"Then have them make a sanctuary for me, and I will dwell among them"* (Exodus 25:8 NIV).[45]

In the New Testament, God continued to demonstrate His desire to be with His people. When Isaiah prophesied about the coming of Jesus Christ, he said, *"Therefore the Lord himself will give you a sign: The virgin will conceive and give birth to a son, and will call him Immanuel"* (Isaiah 7:14 NIV). The name Immanuel means "God with us." (See Matthew 1:23.) And notice what God says in the book of Revelation about His presence with us in the new heavens and earth:

> And I heard a loud voice from the throne saying, "Look! **God's dwelling place is now among the people**, and he will dwell with them. They will be his people, and **God himself will be with them and be their God.** 'He will wipe every tear from their eyes. There will be no more

44. Andrew A. Bonar, ed., *Memoir and Remains of the Reverend Robert Murray M'Cheyne, Minister of St. Peter's Church, Dundee,* reprint ed. (Whitefish, MT: Kessinger Publishing, LLC, 2006; Edinburgh, Scotland: William Oliphant and Co., 1864), 162. Page number refers to the reprint edition.
45. Daniel R. Hyde, "The Ark of the Covenant and God's Presence with Us," Ligonier, September 19, 2012, https://www.ligonier.org/learn/articles/ark-covenant-and-gods-presence-us.

death' or mourning or crying or pain, for the old order of things has passed away." (Revelation 21:3–4 NIV)

When we truly understand that God desires to be present with us, we will not think of Him as a distant deity who is uncaring about or unaware of our fear and anxiety, but we will draw close to Him and give Him all our needs. *"The Lord is close to the brokenhearted and saves those who are crushed in spirit"* (Psalm 34:18 NIV).

WHEN WE TRULY UNDERSTAND THAT GOD DESIRES TO BE PRESENT WITH US, WE WILL DRAW CLOSE TO HIM AND GIVE HIM ALL OUR NEEDS.

GOD'S OMNIPRESENCE AND HIS MANIFEST PRESENCE

It's important to recognize that there are two aspects to God's presence: His omnipresence and His manifest presence. The reality of these two "presences" can be complex, but we need to understand how it impacts our lives.

GOD'S OMNIPRESENCE

IN THE UNIVERSE

God's omnipresence refers to His being everywhere in the universe, all the time. *"'Who can hide in secret places so that I cannot see them?' declares the Lord. 'Do not I fill heaven and earth?' declares the Lord"* (Jeremiah 23:24 NIV).

The omnipresence of God is a reality, whether or not we are aware of it. He is present, with His whole being, at every point in space. The Bible teaches this idea, as expressed in Psalm 139:7–10:

Where shall I go from your Spirit? Or where shall I flee from your presence? If I ascend to heaven, you are there! If I make my bed in

Sheol, you are there! If I take the wings of the morning and dwell in the uttermost parts of the sea, even there your hand shall lead me, and your right hand shall hold me.   (ESV)

Wherever we are in the world, we are never outside the objective and real presence of God.

IN BELIEVERS' HEARTS

In the new covenant provided through Christ, we are reconciled to our heavenly Father. God comes to dwell inside us through the Holy Spirit, and He continues to live within us. God's presence no longer dwells within the ark of the covenant in the holy of holies, where only the high priest could enter, but His Spirit now inhabits these "earthen vessels" of our bodies. (See 2 Corinthians 4:7 KJV.) If you are a genuine, born-again, Spirit-filled believer, His presence now resides in you. His presence in your heart is an objective fact. Whether or not you are aware of God's presence, God is always there.

God's presence and His law are major topics in the Old Testament, and they both find their fullest expression and intention in the new covenant in Christ, through which we receive the gift of regeneration and the indwelling Holy Spirit. The Ten Commandments were inscribed on tablets of stone and placed in the ark of the covenant. But because Jesus has reconciled us to the Father, God's law is now written on the tablets of our hearts, a spiritual reality prophesied by Jeremiah: "'This is the covenant I will make with the people of Israel after that time,' declares the LORD. 'I will put my law in their minds and write it on their hearts. I will be their God, and they will be my people'" (Jeremiah 31:33 NIV).

Building on this prophetic word, the apostle Paul wrote the following captivating words:

You yourselves are our letter, written on our hearts, known and read by everyone. You show that you are a letter from Christ, the result of our ministry, written not with ink but with the Spirit of the living God, not on tablets of stone but on tablets of human hearts. Such confidence we have through Christ before God.   (2 Corinthians 3:2–4 NIV)

GOD'S MANIFEST PRESENCE

God's *manifest* presence refers to His presence made known to us in discernible and personal ways in our lives. For example, we may experience His manifest presence through receiving insights into Scripture, a spiritual gift, a healing, a sudden supernatural courage to meet a challenge, inner joy, or unexplainable peace. Such spiritual realities may be hard for people to understand if they do not have the Holy Spirit living within them (and sometimes even if they do). Many people think God is far away and uninterested in their lives, while others believe He is cold and uncaring. Those mindsets become their *perceived* reality. As Christians, we do not base our faith in the existence and love of God on perceived reality stemming from human reason. We base it on the existential reality attested to by the revealed Word of God and by our personal experiences of God's presence through the indwelling Holy Spirit.

When we experience the manifest presence of God, we have a deep awareness of Him that awakens us to His existential reality. We might think of our present circumstances as our reality. There's some truth to that, but, even more so, God's presence is our defining reality. There is never a time when our heavenly Father is not present with us, but there may be times when He is not manifestly with us. In his famous work *The Pursuit of God*, A. W. Tozer wrote, "The presence and the manifestation of the presence are not the same. There can be one without the other. God is here when we are wholly unaware of it. He is manifest only when and as we are aware of His presence."[46]

In the book of Daniel, we see an example of God manifesting His presence while revealing His omnipresence. We know that the Lord never abandoned Daniel's friends Shadrach, Meshach, and Abednego. But, for a time, it seemed as if the only monarch in their lives was King Nebuchadnezzar—and he was furious at the three Hebrew men, ready to violently execute them for not bowing down to the golden image he had made. Unaware of God's omnipresence, the king thrust the three men into a burning, fiery furnace. That is when God *manifested* His presence. "*King Nebuchadnezzar leaped to his feet in amazement.... He said, 'Look! I see four men walking around in the fire, unbound and unharmed, and the fourth looks*

---

46. "A. W. Tozer Quotes," Goodreads, https://www.goodreads.com/quotes/7212680-the-presence-and-the-manifestation-of-the-presence-are-not.

like a son of the gods'" (Daniel 3:24–25 NIV). The reality of God's existence had become visibly discernible, even to the pagan king. This was God's manifest presence—protecting the three men, preserving them, and even fellowshipping with them during their fiery ordeal.

> **WHEN WE EXPERIENCE THE MANIFEST PRESENCE OF GOD, WE HAVE A DEEP AWARENESS OF HIM THAT AWAKENS US TO HIS EXISTENTIAL REALITY.**

A DRAMATIC STORY ABOUT THE ARK OF THE COVENANT

What does it mean for us that God desires to manifest His presence to and through us in the midst of our fears and anxiety? The following is an imaginary scenario about the ark of the covenant that I hope will give you a sense of the drama and significance connected to God's power residing within you when you face the daunting enemy of fear. I also hope it will give you a glimpse of the reaction of the forces of darkness each time they are faced with the reality of *whose* you are and *what* you possess through God's indwelling presence, so you will be strengthened in your faith and spiritual courage.

The Israelites' enemies are growing restless. They are about to wage war against the Hebrew people, but they are concerned because they know firsthand the overwhelming power that seems to emanate from the ark of the covenant that resides in the Israelites' camp. On the eve of the engagement, a new captain in one of the enemy units debates with the soldiers under his command, several of whom are veterans of many battles, about their chances of victory.

The captain begins by saying, "I'm ready for this fight. But the commanders are saying we could be slaughtered if the Israelites carry this strange, gold-covered wooden box before them at the time of the battle."

One of the soldiers speaks up: "Sir, we've seen what this strange box does to those who dare to threaten the ones who possess it. The power that abides within it somehow lays waste to anyone who stands against those who carry it! You should not underestimate it."

The captain asks, "Has anyone seen the contents of this box?"

The soldier replies, "No, sir, but we've heard rumors!"

"What kind of rumors?"

"Sir, I am not sure if it is true or not, but we've heard that this box hides the so-called tablets of stone on which Moses inscribed the commandments of Israel's God."

The captain is curious and asks, "What else?"

"They say it contains a staff."

"A staff? What kind of staff?"

"Sir, it's more like a branch or piece of wood or a walking stick that has flowers budding out of the top of it. It's said to be the same staff Moses used to part the Red Sea!"

As some of the newer soldiers standing around the captain work unsuccessfully to conceal their laughter, their captain shouts, "Silence, all of you! What else does the Israelite army possess in the box?"

A bit hesitantly, the first soldier responds, "Well, sir, it's said that there is a jar filled with a substance they claim fed them in the wilderness when we thought we had them surrounded under siege."

The captain quickly asks, "What is this substance?"

"They call it 'manna.'"

"'Manna'? What does that signify?"

Again, with a tinge of hesitancy, the soldier says, "Sir, please understand, I am not mocking you when I give my answer. The name means 'What is it?'"

One of the other soldiers rises to his feet and shouts, "It's as if their God taunts us!"

The captain scoffs. "There is no way that two pieces of inscribed stone, a simple wooden staff, and a jar of this so-called 'What is it?' resting in a wooden box could possibly give the Israelites special power."

"No, Captain!" the first soldier says. "That's the thing. They do not claim these elements give them *any* power at all. They claim the secret of their 'God box' is...."

"Well?"

"It's hard to say this, sir, but please remember that these are their words, not mine!"

Frustrated, the captain shouts, "Get on with it! What is the secret of this God box?"

"Sir, they say it contains the supernatural presence of their God!"

Infuriated, the captain jumps to his feet and screams, "That's foolishness! Does their God dwell in a box made of wood covered with gold?"

Cautiously, the soldier reminds the captain, "Sir, with all due respect, we've lost thousands of our men because of this God box. It is as if an unrestricted power goes before and behind the Israelites, as long as this *box* remains in their possession. The truth is, no matter how many men we send with swords, spears, and shields, even with our best chariots and drivers, we cannot defeat them. As long as they possess this God box, we cannot win! We cannot even disquiet them. They go on singing and rejoicing—even dancing!"

The captain looks out over the encampment of armies, lost in thought, taking in everything the seasoned soldier has told him.

After a little while, he exhales, and his words erupt from him with a hint of desperation: "Then we will steal the God box!"

"Pardon me, sir?" the first soldier says.

"I said, then we will take it!"

The brave soldier replies, "Sir, with all due respect, how can we even get near where the Israelites live, much less capture this God box? As long as they have this box that contains their God's presence, I fear we will be defeated!"

The soldiers await the captain's next response, but there is only silence. The accounts of the Israelites' God have convinced him of the Deity's supreme power and willingness to defend and protect His people. And now the captain is worried too…

I've taken the liberty of dramatizing a story about the ark of the covenant as if it were straight out of a movie script. Yet the ark itself and its history are not fiction or myth but reality. (See, for example, Exodus 25:10–22; 37:1–9; Joshua 3; 2 Chronicles 35:1–19.) The Israelites' peace and protection were not predicated on their own presence or ability but solely on God's presence, which went before them, with them, and behind them. As the psalmist wrote, *"You hem me in behind and before, and you lay your hand upon me"* (Psalm 139:5 NIV).

As long as the Israelites stayed in fellowship with God and obeyed His Word, then His presence and power went before them, defeating all their enemies. Unfortunately, that was not always the case. When they disobeyed God, even having the ark with them did not give them success. At one point, the Philistines even captured the ark of the covenant. (See 1 Samuel 4.) This shows us that the ark was not "magic." It was where God chose to manifest His presence, but it was not the same as His presence.

ISRAEL'S PEACE AND PROTECTION WERE NOT PREDICATED ON THEIR OWN PRESENCE OR ABILITY BUT SOLELY ON GOD'S PRESENCE, WHICH WENT BEFORE THEM, WITH THEM, AND BEHIND THEM.

THE GIFT OF PEACE

The above scenario depicts what Israel's enemies felt like when they found themselves facing the creative Power that rested in the ark of the covenant. Their reaction is similar to how the forces of darkness feel each time they come to incite you with fear or anxiety but find you filled with God's peace, resting in His indwelling presence. We can live in peace, joy, and victory even during the most troubling times when we know our heavenly Father is near and is in control of all that happens in this world. The demonic powers dread the manifestation of God's peace in our lives because they recognize they can no longer use the instrument of fear to distract or control us.

> *Even though I walk through the valley of the shadow of death, I fear no evil, for **You are with me**; Your rod and Your staff, they comfort me.*
> (Psalm 23:4 NASB)

The presence of God is like a security blanket, covering us with His love and peace, and protecting us with His right arm of power. The rod in the ark of the covenant once represented God's supernatural ability, but today we look to God's mighty power in the resurrection of Jesus Christ from the dead and our rebirth in Him. No longer does the jar filled with manna represent God's provision because Jesus is the Bread of Heaven who dwells within us, sustaining us and providing spiritual food for every wilderness experience of our lives. (See, for example, John 6:51.)

Know this: because God dwells within you by His Spirit, the darkness has no power over you. Christ is your Savior, and you are protected on every side. Fear, anxiety, worry, and dismay lose their potency as you experience God's manifest presence. All inward discord and doubt are banished. God's peace safeguards and insulates you from all that threatens or opposes His purposes for your life and future. *"And the peace of God, which transcends all understanding, will guard your hearts and your minds in Christ Jesus"* (Philippians 4:7 NIV).

We have been given the gift of peace with God and peace with self, including the repose and pleasure of having a mind directed by God's counsel and love. Such a peace, Paul wrote, *"transcends"* all human reasoning. It can be known only as an inner experience by the believer who is connected to the heavenly Father.

Millions of people suffer needlessly from fear, panic, and anxiety, not because the peace of God isn't available, but because they have never been taught that the Prince of Peace wants to reign supreme in their hearts and lives. The secret to peace is not outside you but within you—because the presence of God is there. You can access this peace as you daily surrender your life to the Lord and His purposes, worship Him, bring all your needs to Him in prayer, and stand on the promises in His Word. In the next chapter, we will talk specifically about the power of God's Word to protect and defend us.

The peace of God that abides in our hearts is a sure, trustworthy fortress. It is our duty as spiritual warriors to guard that peace against the evil one who seeks to destroy it. Determine that you will not settle for another day of living in fear. Keep the river of God's presence and peace flowing through you, no matter what schemes the enemy uses against you. Choose to follow and serve God all the days of your life. Decide now that you will maintain an intimate relationship with your heavenly Father, for there is peace in that secret place of intimacy.

10

THE FATHER'S INSTRUCTIONS

"In tribulation immediately draw near to God with confidence,
and you will receive strength, enlightenment, and instruction."
—*John of the Cross*[47]

A few years ago, one of my associates and I were called to visit someone gravely ill in a medical center here in California. As we entered the facility, I asked a young man near the front desk to direct me to the ward where the patient was being treated. The young man quickly turned and replied, "Sure! Go to the second floor, turn right, then make a left and walk right through Unit Q's two large doors."

Something about this young man's instructions didn't feel right. So, as we exited the elevator, I marched directly to the nurse's station, where a young lady was standing, and repeated the man's instructions for verification.

The moment I finished telling her what we had been instructed to do, the young woman's appearance went from an expression of happiness to one of terror; she looked as if all the blood had drained out of her face.

---

47. "John of the Cross Quotes," Goodreads, https://www.goodreads.com/author/
quotes/19568117.John_of_the_Cross.

She gasped, then asked, "Who gave you those instructions, again?" I told her it was the young man downstairs. She quickly picked up the phone, called the downstairs front desk, and bellowed, "Who gave these gentlemen instructions to enter Unit Q?"

After listening for a moment, she hung up the phone and began apologizing profusely, saying, "I am so sorry, gentlemen. The young man you spoke to was just released from his job. It is the third time he's jeopardized our staff and visitors."

I asked, "How so?"

She replied, "The unit he directed you to is a highly quarantined area. Had you entered that place, you would have been subject to isolation because you likely would have been exposed to a highly contagious outbreak that occurred here in the area. Unfortunately, four other people were mistakenly directed there, and one of them contracted the disease, resulting in his being admitted to that ward. The other three had to stay three nights in a clearance area until we were sure they were safe to leave."

Within seconds, I was reminded of just how powerful and dangerous instructions can be. If we had followed the directions of the newly unemployed young man, it could have cost us precious time and, worse, our health or even our lives!

Thankfully, a young woman who understood the power of proper directions had intervened. As a result, we safely accomplished what we had gone to the hospital to do. Following the right instructions matters!

INTENTIONAL INSTRUCTIONS WITH GUARANTEED RESULTS

Perhaps the most potent principle we can discover in learning how to live a fear-free life is to understand the difference between common words of instruction and specialized instructions that are infused with God's preserving power. Let me explain.

Directions are a natural form of describing for someone how something should be done. They are often given without any proof of the eventual outcome or the potential consequences of failing to follow through. Unlike directions, which tend to be general navigational cues, instructions are detailed and hold a tone of authority when delivered, even though, if they are flawed due to inaccuracy, they may produce results that fall short of what was desired.

Again, in the natural, instructions come without any guarantees that what you have been directed to do will work. There are no absolute assurances that your actions will produce tangible, fail-proof results, such as security, power, and preservation.

Unlike human-issued directions, God's instructions are backed, supported, and secured by the total forces and resources of heaven! Corrie ten Boom said, "Don't bother to give God instructions; just report for duty."[48] Blessed are those who listen to His instructions and obey. In the book of Proverbs, "Wisdom" exhorts:

> And now, O sons, listen to me: blessed are those who keep my ways. **Hear instruction and be wise, and do not neglect it.** Blessed is the one who listens to me, watching daily at my gates, waiting beside my doors. **For whoever finds me** finds life and obtains favor from the LORD, **but he who fails to find me** injures himself; all who hate me love death.
>
> (Proverbs 8:32–36 ESV)

In his commentary notes on this passage, theologian Albert Barnes describes verse 32 as "the old exhortation with a new force. The counsels are no longer those of prudence and human experience, but of a Wisdom eternal of Yahweh, ordering all things."[49]

In short, God's kind of instructions bring supernatural favor, power, preservation, and provision! They also cancel out any chance of error or misdirection that would lead you into jeopardy or, worse, something from which you cannot escape. Let's look at some significant ways in which we can apply this principle to our lives.

---

48. "Corrie ten Boom Quotes," Goodreads, https://www.goodreads.com/author/quotes/102203.Corrie_ten_Boom.
49. Albert Barnes, "Notes on the Bible by Albert Barnes [1834]," https://biblehub.com/proverbs/8-33.htm.

THE FATHER'S INSTRUCTIONS REMOVE FEAR

Reflecting on my life, I cannot begin to tell you how many times my earthly father's instructions saved me! His words concerning what to do when under attack have proven helpful in far more situations than merely warring against wild animals or dogs. They have taught me what to do when facing trials and oppositions, in both the natural and the spirit. Most of all, they have secured me. My father's voice of instruction still guides and preserves me, even years after his passing. Interestingly, I can hear his voice along with the voice of my heavenly Father as I read the book of Proverbs and all the other life-preserving books of the Bible.

Because I listened to and retained my father's instructions, I have saved myself countless hours of needless pain, frustration, and fear. Those lessons have fortified me over the years and taught me what to do and what not to do.

WORDS THAT PROTECT AND PRESERVE

In similar ways, our heavenly Father's instructions safeguard and maintain us. The wisdom, direction, and instructions found in the pages of God's Word are life-giving and lifesaving. The writer of Proverbs was correct in saying that this kind of wisdom not only preserves our lives but also secures our hearts with the confidence that when we walk in it, we are safe.

In that peaceful place established by the heavenly Father's wisdom, fear finds no place in our hearts. Intimidation holds no power over those who walk in their Father's instructions. Why? Because hell knows well that God's instructions have heaven's backing and the Holy Spirit's power. As children of the King, we have everything we need to withstand Satan's deceit and schemes.

WORDS WITH UNPARALLELED POWER

There is a supernatural aspect to the kind of instructions we receive from the Lord. Carefully read the following two verses, because there is spiritual power in words!

It is the Spirit who gives life; the flesh conveys no benefit [it is of no account]. The words I have spoken to you are spirit and life [providing eternal life]. (John 6:63 AMP)

For the word of God is living and active, sharper than any two-edged sword, piercing to the division of soul and of spirit, of joints and of marrow, and discerning the thoughts and intentions of the heart. (Hebrews 4:12 ESV)

"Words create worlds," as Rabbi Abraham Joshua Heschel described.[50] As we previously discussed, at the beginning of the world, God spoke words, and there was creative power in those words that made the earth in all its splendor. Similarly, the breath of God's words brings a life-giving force into your spirit. The Word of God is not passive but active; it is a living thing that pierces the soul and spirit, capturing every intention of the heart, as expressed by the above verse from Hebrews.

God's instructions flow to the pierced heart, bringing faith that conquers fear. His instructions, given through His Word, are more than a compilation of mere human sentences or vernacular statements. They are creative, infused with supernatural power!

Everything written whose source is God is a living oracle made possible by the breath of God, is divinely inspired, and can prove profitable in multiple ways. God's words of instruction carry the supernatural ability to reveal, rebuke, correct, restore, and, yes, secure us! *"All Scripture is God-breathed and is useful for teaching, rebuking, correcting and training in righteousness, so that the servant of God may be thoroughly equipped for every good work"* (2 Timothy 3:16–17 NIV).

GOD'S INSTRUCTIONS ENABLE US TO STAND IN FAITH

I have previously mentioned the need to stand in faith. You might think the mere act of standing would pose no real threat to the spirit of fear, but it does. That is why the Bible instructs us to stand in faith against

---

50. "Abraham Joshua Heschel Quotes," Goodreads, https://www.goodreads.com/quotes/10670103-words-create-worlds.

the enemy. In Ephesians 6:11–13, the apostle Paul outlines the following instructions for wielding spiritual weapons against the rulers of darkness:

> *Put on the whole armor of God, that you may be able to **stand against** the wiles of the devil. For we wrestle not **against** flesh and blood, but **against** principalities, **against** powers, **against** the rulers of the darkness of this world, **against** spiritual wickedness in high places. Wherefore take to you the whole armor of God, that you may be able to **withstand** in the evil day, and having done all, to **stand**.* (KJVER)

Within these words from Paul is perhaps one of the most overlooked principles in the Bible related to fear-free living. Notice the apostle's use of the words *stand* and *against* in this text. Paul, who himself had discovered the power of "standing," uses the word *stand* twice and the word *against* six times, in the King James Version. There is a reason for this, which I will illustrate with the following story.

STAND TALL—YOUR LIFE DEPENDS ON IT!

A few years ago, I traveled to Alaska and was invited to join a group on a salmon fishing excursion. The trip required us to travel by stream back into the deep interior of the state, hundreds of miles away from roads or civilization. When we approached the place where we were scheduled to be dropped off with our armed fishing guide (a detail that should have alerted us to the gravity of what we were getting ourselves into in the first place), we were given our fishing gear, a roll of duct tape, and the following instructions: "In the unlikely event you are approached by a grizzly bear, remain calm. Lay your fishing rod down, along with the fish you've caught, and attempt to slowly back away." It sounded reasonable enough—until we heard this addendum: "If one of these bears attempts to charge you, your only hope of surviving will be to stand straight up, making yourself appear as tall as possible; raise your hands as high as you can; and scream at the top of your lungs, 'Hey, bear!'" The guide explained that such actions would make the bear think we were as large as itself and that we were not afraid, and would then back off. (This reminded me of my father's "HASH BROWN!" advice!)

The guide continued, "When and if the bear does back off, take your fish, calmly walk away to where you are safe, and change your underwear!" We all began to laugh, but the guide quickly added, "I'm not kidding."

As we drew nearer to the location where we would fish, I inquired, "By the way, what is the duct tape for?" The guide replied, "I almost forgot! If these bears do attack you, they usually begin by swiping their large claws across the top of the head. If this happens, when you regain consciousness, you'll take the tape and wrap your scalp back on to help stop the bleeding before calmly seeking assistance." We laughed again, thinking our guide was having some fun at our expense. He quickly assured us that he was not. He concluded by saying, "More people have been saved by standing tall against these animals than by those who ended up using the duct tape. Standing up as tall as you can and screaming as loud as you can, if attacked, can save your life!"

STAND AGAINST, AND BE BRAVE

My experience in Alaska reminds me of the power inscribed into the words of the apostle Paul's message from Ephesians 6. Stand! When you have done all that you can do, stand some more! Interestingly, the Greek word translated "*stand*" in verses 11 and 13 is *histēmi* (pronounced his'-tay-mee) and means to "abide" in such a way as to hold up, establish a presence. Its meaning is rooted in the idea of making a stand, setting yourself against an aggressive force, especially in the company of others. It means to make and remain firm or to be fixed and established; to cause a person or a thing to keep its place or remain intact, such as a kingdom or a family; and to escape safely.[51]

Even more powerful is the following meaning attached to all of it: when we stand, it is not a natural stance in our authority or power. This kind of standing is secured and enforced by the powers of heaven. Our standing firm in faith is upheld and sustained by the authority and force of God and all His armies! (It kind of cancels out the need for duct tape!)

Keeping all this in mind, consider God's instructions to Moses in Exodus 14:13: "*Don't be afraid. Stand firm and watch GOD do his work of*

---

51. *Strong's*, #2476, https://www.bibletools.org/index.cfm/fuseaction/Lexicon.show/ID/G2476/histemi.htm.

salvation for you today" (MSG). Paul's words in Ephesians 6:11 are reminiscent of those: *"Put on all of God's armor so that you will be able to stand firm against all strategies of the devil"* (Ephesians 6:11 NLT).

I am also reminded of Psalm 91, which paints a picture of the way God protects and shelters those who trust in Him. It is worth reading through the entirety of this psalm:

> *He that dwells in the secret place of the Most High shall abide under the shadow of the Almighty. I will say of the LORD, He is my refuge and my fortress: my God; in Him will I trust. Surely He shall deliver you from the snare of the fowler, and from the noisome pestilence. He shall cover you with His feathers, and under His wings shall you trust: His truth shall be your shield and buckler. You shall not be afraid for the terror by night; nor for the arrow that flies by day; nor for the pestilence that walks in darkness; nor for the destruction that wastes at noonday. A thousand shall fall at your side, and ten thousand at your right hand; but it shall not come near you. Only with your eyes shall you behold and see the reward of the wicked. Because you have made the LORD, which is my refuge, even the Most High, your habitation; there shall no evil befall you, neither shall any plague come near your dwelling. For He shall give His angels charge over you, to keep you in all your ways. They shall bear you up in their hands, lest you dash your foot against a stone. You shall tread upon the lion and adder: the young lion and the dragon shall you trample under feet. Because he has set his love upon Me, therefore will I deliver him: I will set him on high, because he has known My name. He shall call upon Me, and I will answer him: I will be with him in trouble; I will deliver him, and honor him. With long life will I satisfy him, and show him My salvation.*
>
> (Psalm 91 KJVER)

WHERE WILL YOU STAND?

There is a big difference between standing in our own strength and standing in the confidence, strength, and power of the presence of our heavenly Father and King. When we stand in His presence, His shadow overpowers and superimposes itself over unease, worry, anxiety, fear, alarm, and distress. No wonder David, having experienced this supernatural protection firsthand, wrote these words:

> *Even though I walk through the valley of the shadow of death, I fear no*
> *evil, for You are with me; Your rod and Your staff, they comfort me.*
> *You prepare a table before me in the presence of my enemies; You have*
> *anointed my head with oil; my cup overflows. Certainly, goodness and*
> *faithfulness will follow me all the days of my life, and my dwelling will*
> *be in the house of the LORD forever.*   (Psalm 23:4–6 NASB)

Like David did, you can acquire supernatural courage and unflagging confidence when you know that your heavenly Father stands with, over, behind, and before you in every threatening situation and circumstance! God has made it clear that no one can stand against His people. Just as He said to Joshua, "*No one will be able to stand against you all the days of your life. As I was with Moses, so I will be with you; I will never leave you nor forsake you*" (Joshua 1:5 NIV).

Life's challenges are real, not imaginary battles. There should be no doubt in our minds that Satan will attempt to strike fear in our hearts with every test he throws our way. The good news is that fear loses its power when we stand in the confidence of God's presence and preserving power, not our own. Finally, when battles appear, God's presence will turn them into victories when we choose to stand our ground in and with *Him*.

SAY SOMETHING!

God has instructed us on how to stand in His strength and resist the enemy's attacks. But how do we maintain our confidence in His presence and power? One key is to speak His powerful Word aloud, declaring His promises and reminding ourselves verbally of His presence. A dear friend of mine, Bishop Joseph Garlington, shared a powerful message a few years ago entitled "Nothing Happens in the Kingdom Until You Say Something!" In one of his most famous sermon series, he shared how God's creative power is released into the atmosphere to change natural realities when we openly dare to declare God's promises in and over our lives!

The words we speak are sounds caused by air passing through our larynxes, verbalizing thoughts into sentences and phrases; but in the spiritual realm, words are synonymous with creative power. In the human realm, words often represent little more than a statement, question, or promise, but in the spiritual realm, God's words do more than convey information; they are creative. His words become what He speaks. When you speak God's words, they have power!

Nothing happens in the kingdom until you dare to use words to declare God's power and affirm what He has spoken. This principle reminds me of the story of the centurion in Matthew 8. It begins like this:

> *And when Jesus was entered into Capernaum, there came to Him a centurion, beseeching Him, and saying, Lord, my servant lies at home sick of the palsy, grievously tormented. And Jesus says to him, I will come and heal him.* (Matthew 8:5–7 KJVER)

Sometimes, a profound word can be revealed through a seemingly unlikely person. This centurion, acquainted with the strength of military might and authority, next spoke these words to Jesus: *"Lord, I am not worthy that You should come under my roof: but speak the word only, and my servant shall be healed"* (Matthew 8:8 KJVER).

"Speak the word only"—what a shocking statement for a centurion to make. His reasoning went as follows: *"For I am a man under authority, having soldiers under me: and I say to this man, Go, and he goes; and to another, Come, and he comes; and to my servant, Do this, and he does it"* (verse 9 KJVER).

Jesus recognized this man's faith in the power of His words, and He responded accordingly: *"When Jesus heard it, He marveled, and said to them that followed, Verily I say to you, I have not found so great faith, no, not in Israel"* (verse 10 KJVER).

The results of Jesus's words are amazing. *"Jesus said to the centurion, Go your way; and as you have believed, so be it done to you. And his servant was healed in the selfsame hour"* (verse 13 KJVER).

No doubt, the centurion in this story was extremely concerned about his servant and wanted to do something to prolong the man's life. Only one word from Jesus replaced his fears and concerns with supernatural resolve. In an instant, his servant went from fighting for his life to rejoicing over his immediate healing. Just imagine how the powers of darkness react as we speak God's Word when confronted by fearful circumstances and intimidating challenges!

GOD'S WORD CHANGES ATMOSPHERES

I will never forget how quickly the atmosphere shifted when I heard my father's voice joined with mine in the presence of those lunging dogs I talked about in chapter 1. My circumstances were suddenly altered when my father's words merged with mine, and mine with his. Interestingly, while I was yelling and waving my arms, it was my father's voice and words that chased off the violent aggressors!

Similarly, fear loses its grip when we speak the words of our heavenly Father. When the dark powers of the underworld hear our Father's words in our mouths, it's as if He is the one speaking them. As we speak His Word, we become conduits of His Spirit and authority, not our own. When we become representatives of His power, we cause every form of fear to shudder and run for cover!

Therefore, whenever we feel fear approaching, we need to speak God's Word. Whenever we sense the ungoverned emotion or unnatural spirit of fear working to paralyze us, we must remember the power we have to rebuke and refute the evil one by quoting, repeating, and echoing our Father's promises for our lives and futures. Let's be sure to speak boldly, believing wholeheartedly that God will fulfill His Word.

There have been thousands of occasions when I've heard or sensed a threat coming out of Satan's ugly old jowls. But I've discovered a secret: I don't wait until fear has its foot in my door. Instead, I slam the door in the devil's face, declaring, "Satan, you are a liar. You have no power here. You have no authority here. You have no legal right even to approach or address me! I am who God says I am. I have what He says I have. I will be who He says I am. God said it, I believe it, and that settles it!" Then I drive him back even further with the weapon of my Father's Word, either quoting directly from Scripture or declaring a paraphrase. I may say, for example,

"Greater is He who lives within me than he who is in the world! I am a child of God, so I have overcome you and anything you might use against me!" Even paraphrasing these powerful words from 1 John 4:4 makes the devil quake in his nasty socks.

The enemy will never relent until you learn to stand up against him and speak the Word. My wife, Jordana, and I have had moments when it felt as if we were being surrounded on every side by the enemy. But it was in those moments that God's Word proved to be lethal to everything he had sent to harm us as we prayed and declared such fear-defeating passages as Psalm 56:3–4: "*When I am afraid, I will put my trust in You. In God, whose word I praise, in God I have put my trust; I shall not be afraid. What can mere mortals do to me?*" (NASB).

I can remember many a night when we discovered heavenly couriers of strength and solace by simply quoting these fear-defeating passages.

Years ago, I was going through what felt like one of the most threatening seasons of my life. I had received a negative report via email concerning my body. And although I was standing in faith and refusing to acknowledge or accept it, Satan still used the situation as an opportunity to hitch a ride on the words of that report, attempting to gain a stronghold in my heart and mind.

I can still recall the feeling of terror and anxiety that threatened to overcome me the first night after I'd read those discouraging words. I was fighting my emotions. I could sense the presence of unauthorized spirits waiting to jump on anything through which I might have given them access. It was as if I could hear the devil's voice saying, "Finally, I've got you where I want you. There is no escape! I am going to take you out!"

At first, I tried to ignore these thoughts and go to sleep. But, that night, I wrestled with my emotions until the early morning, tossing and turning, working to outsmart and outmuscle them. Then I came to a clear, powerfully defined realization: "Mark, you're not going to whip this thing with wit, words, or human strength! You'd better get up and pull out your sword of the Spirit from its sheath!"

I knew this law of spiritual warfare: we do not fight against flesh and blood but against principalities, powers of darkness, and rulers in high places. (See Ephesians 6:12.) I've heard it said there are some battles you can't fight by yourself in your flesh. However, I disagree, because I have discovered you cannot fight *one single battle* without the assistance of the Spirit of God, the Word of God, and the blood of Jesus.

So, I sat straight up in bed, turned on the bedside lamp, grabbed my Bible, and began to address every demon lurking in my room by boldly declaring, out loud, these forceful words from Psalm 27:

> *The LORD is my light and my salvation; whom shall I fear? the LORD is the strength of my life; of whom shall I be afraid? When the wicked, even my enemies and my foes, came upon me to eat up my flesh, they stumbled and fell. Though a host should encamp against me, my heart shall not fear: though war should rise against me, in this will I be confident. One thing have I desired of the LORD, that will I seek after; that I may dwell in the house of the LORD all the days of my life, to behold the beauty of the LORD, and to inquire in His temple. For in the time of trouble He shall hide me in His pavilion: in the secret of His tabernacle shall He hide me; He shall set me up upon a rock. And now shall my head be lifted up above my enemies round about me: therefore will I offer in His tabernacle sacrifices of joy; I will sing, yea, I will sing praises to the LORD. Hear, O LORD, when I cry with my voice: have mercy also upon me, and answer me. When You said, Seek you My face; my heart said to You, Your face, LORD, will I seek.*
>
> (Psalm 27:1–8 KJVER)

I wasn't even through the first three verses when I began sensing those demonic spirits dashing for the doors and windows of my emotions and my house. I continued reading aloud from the Psalms, and by the time I reached the end of Psalm 46, every evil spirit had lifted off me and left the room.

> *God is our refuge and strength, a very present help in trouble. Therefore we will not fear though the earth gives way, though the mountains be moved into the heart of the sea, though its waters roar and foam, though the mountains tremble at its swelling.* (Psalm 46:1–3 ESV)

As peace filled my heart and rest came over my body, mind, will, and emotions, I heard the Holy Spirit say, "Don't stop just yet!" So, I quoted the Word from Isaiah 41:13: *"For I, the LORD your God, hold your right hand; it is I who say to you, 'Fear not, I am the one who helps you'"* (ESV).

Then I read Jesus's words in John 14:27: *"Peace I leave with you; my peace I give to you. Not as the world gives do I give to you. Let not your hearts be troubled, neither let them be afraid"* (ESV).

Just as I was falling asleep, I heard, "Mark, let's leave these spirits something they can worry about!" So, I read and prayed Psalm 91:4–5. As I lay on my back, I held my Bible above my face and repeated these words: *"He shall cover you with His feathers, and under His wings shall you trust: His truth shall be your shield and buckler. You shall not be afraid for the terror by night; nor for the arrow that flies by day."*

When I awoke the following day, it was as if my room had experienced a thorough deep cleansing. Every web of fear and anxiety had been pulled from the gorges of my mind, will, and emotions, as if our entire home had been swept clean and fumigated to keep spiritual spiders, rats, and snakes from ever returning.

The following week, I received another letter from my physician, part of which read, "Dear Mark, You no longer have to be concerned! You are clean! There is no trace of disease in your body!" I lifted my hands and worshipped God with Jordana!

I can't count the number of times God's Word has worked to chase the enemy's threats out of our lives, as well as to bring newfound peace, courage, and healing that surpassed all human understanding. The next time you feel threatened or fearful, grab the sword of the Spirit and use it! In Deuteronomy 3:22, Moses said to Joshua about the opposition he would face in the promised land, *"You shall not fear them, for it is the LORD your God who fights for you"* (ESV).

PRAY IN THE SPIRIT

Another powerful weapon we can use against fear, angst, and even exasperation is the very prayers of the Spirit, who bears our burdens, comforting and spiritually reinforcing us. Paul wrote about how the Spirit assists us in our weaknesses:

In the same way, the Spirit [comes to us and] helps us in our weakness. We do not know what prayer to offer or how to offer it as we should, but the Spirit Himself [knows our need and at the right time] intercedes on our behalf with sighs and groanings too deep for words. And He who searches the hearts knows what the mind of the Spirit is, because the Spirit intercedes [before God] on behalf of God's people in accordance with God's will. (Romans 8:26–27 AMP)

One Bible commentary beautifully conveys the ideas in this passage:

"As we struggle to express in articulate language the desires of our hearts and find that our deepest emotions are the most inexpressible, we 'groan' under this felt inability. But not in vain are these groanings. For 'the Spirit Himself' is in them, giving to the emotions which He Himself has kindled the only language of which they are capable."[52]

That language is the language of the Spirit, which is a gift to us. You are not alone in your prayers, for the Spirit makes intercession for you. Even more, there is a duality of prayer partners that we are mostly unaware of: Christ and the Spirit: *"It is Christ who died, and furthermore is also risen, who is even at the right hand of God, who also makes intercession for us"* (Romans 8:34 NKJV).

As if this isn't powerful enough, God instills in us the supernatural courage and confidence needed to secure peace in His plans for our future. *"**And we know** [with great confidence] that God [who is deeply concerned about us] causes all things to work together [as a plan] for good for those who love God, to those who are called according to His plan and purpose"* (Romans 8:28 AMP).

The Holy Spirit has you covered! The Bible tells us that when we don't know how to pray, or when we feel like we can't find the words to express what we need, then our cries, groans, and utterances in the natural are

52. Jamieson-Fausset-Brown Bible Commentary, https://biblehub.com/commentaries/romans/8-26.htm.

transformed from a natural language to the language of the Spirit, an eternal vernacular that can be neither interrupted nor understood by the forces of darkness!

It is a secret code that not only carries our prayers to God but also unlocks the resources of heaven's vaults, opening spiritual gates and inviting the heavenly hosts to help us in times of need. What a powerful gift!

Fear has no hold on those who have heaven's forces at their signaled call. Make no mistake about it, for there will be moments in your life when you suddenly feel surrounded or, worse, find yourself at the mercy of whatever comes your way. As a born-again, Spirit-filled child of God, you have a direct line, an emergency line, or a hotline, if you will, to heaven—a connection straight from your thoughts to the ears of the Holy Spirit, who in turn translates those cares and concerns into answers. All you need to do is activate this power and then call on Jesus, the Author and Finisher of your faith. (See Hebrews 12:2.) As the Bible says, *"Whosoever shall call upon the name of the Lord shall be saved"* (Romans 10:13 KJV, KJVER).

Your most basic heavenly instruction of all is to call on God's name. Then you must cling to His Word and stand on all its promises, so that the devil will flee. In the next chapter, we will explore what it means to call on the name of our Jesus our Savior to defeat fear.

11

SAY THE NAME OF JESUS

"Great names come and go, but the name of Jesus remains. The devil still hates it, the world still opposes it, but God still blesses it and we can still claim it! 'In the name of Jesus' is the key that unlocks the door of prayer and the treasury of God's grace. It's the weapon that defeats the enemy and the motivation that compels our sacrifice and service. It's the name that causes our hearts to rejoice and our lips to sing his praise."
—*Warren W. Wiersbe*[53]

Another essential facet of living a fear-free life is understanding the power of Jesus's name and calling on Him to deliver us. There are countless stories of people who turned to Jesus in times of fear, crying out, "Jesus, come help me!" and He rescued them. The following is one of those stories.

---

53. Warren W. Wiersbe, *The Names of Jesus* (Grand Rapids, MI: Baker Books, 1997), https://books.google.com/books?id=uYGxXikcUywC&pg=PT102&lpg=PT102&dq=Great+names+come+and+go,+but+the+name+of+Jesus+remains.

In the early 1950s, a small, elderly woman who attended a church in the town where my parents grew up testified how God miraculously saved her life one night from what would have been a violent assault and robbery. She said she had come home as usual after the church's weekly prayer meeting, but as she placed her Bible on the dining room table, preparing to begin her nightly bedtime routine, she heard a noise.

"I thought it was simply the wind or something. It was summertime," she explained. "I always leave my bedroom window open. And because my small apartment sits on the second floor, I didn't think anything about it. So, I picked my Bible back up and made my way to my bedroom to change into my nightgown. But as I walked into my bedroom toward my night table to turn the light on, I heard the door behind me slam shut!"

In recalling that scary night, she said, "Suddenly, two angry voices shouted out of the dimly lit area, 'Lady, put those books down, take off your clothes, and don't say a word or we'll beat you to death!'"

The elderly woman continued, "All I could think of was the name of Jesus! So, I screamed, 'In the name of Jesus! Satan, the Lord rebukes you!' The moment I said, 'In the name of Jesus,' I was shocked when the two men began to scream and pull their legs up as if their feet were on fire! Still not knowing what else to do, I again screamed, 'In the name of Jesus!'"

Suddenly, the men began to shout, "Call them off! Call them off!" Hardly believing her ears, she reached for the phone, dialed her neighbor across the hall, and urged, "Call the police! I am being robbed!" As she hung up the phone and held her Bible to her chest, the men began to beg her, "Please, lady! Please let us go! We won't tell anyone! Just call your dogs off!"

She said that each time they tried to position themselves where they could reach the door handle to escape, "it was if something drove them back into the corner where they almost appeared as if they were trying to climb the bedroom wall." Minutes later, she heard a crash at her front door and a man's voice shouting, "It's the police! We're coming in! Put your weapons down and lie on the floor, now!"

"THE MOMENT I SAID, 'IN THE NAME OF JESUS,' I WAS SHOCKED WHEN THE TWO MEN BEGAN TO SCREAM AND PULL THEIR LEGS UP AS IF THEIR FEET WERE ON FIRE!"

Suddenly, two police officers opened the bedroom door, threw both men to the floor, and speedily placed them in handcuffs. The woman said that one of the thieves began to scream and cry as if he had lost his mind. The other started to shake and weep uncontrollably, saying, "I've been bitten! I'm bleeding! Please take us to the hospital!"

When the police led the would-be robbers out through the door of the second-floor apartment, the woman heard one of the thieves say, "Thank God you guys got here! That woman's dogs almost ate us alive!" As the door closed, one of the policemen said, "You must be high!"

Later, the woman learned that after the arresting officers booked and processed the two men into jail, one of them had to be released and taken to a mental ward. It wasn't until the following week, when the police came back to finish interviewing her for their report, that this petite, elderly woman learned what had caused the men to retreat in terror. After the two arresting officers arrived at her apartment and sat down, one of them said, "Ma'am, we are glad you are okay, but we have to ask you a few more questions."

"Absolutely," she replied.

The officer continued, "Ma'am, first of all, we need to tell you how lucky you are! These men are violent criminals who have raped and robbed many times before." He added, "The last two victims weren't so lucky. One died from the injuries inflicted by these monsters."

Feeling a surge of compassion, she said, "I am so sorry to hear this! That's horrible!"

As the second officer turned a page on his report pad, he asked her something that mystified her. "Ma'am, we only have one more question, and then we will be done and the record will be complete. How long have you had your dogs?"

"Dogs?" she replied.

Perplexed by her response, he said, "Yes, ma'am. Your dogs. How long have you had them?"

Still confused by his statement, she answered, "Please forgive me, officer! I don't understand!"

Trying to get to the bottom of the incident, the officer replied, "Ma'am, we're talking about your bulldogs! The men said they were driven into the corner and held there for nearly thirty minutes by your two large bulldogs." He quickly added, "Ma'am, I assure you, we aren't going to do anything to your dogs or take them away. We just need to see them."

The elderly woman said, "Officer, I don't own any dogs."

The officer asserted, "Ma'am, one of the men we arrested—I mean, the one who still seems to have his mind—swears that two large white bulldogs attacked and held them at bay when you gave the command!"

"What command?" she asked.

With a hint of frustration, he said, "The one you kept giving while you were on the phone with your neighbor."

She tried to figure out what the officers were talking about, but then one of them explained, "The men said that when you shouted 'In the name of Jesus!' your dogs appeared as if out of nowhere and charged them. Both believed they had been bitten and mauled. Both were pleading to be escorted to the emergency room. But when we inspected them, neither of them showed any physical signs of injury. None whatsoever!"

Continuing to clarify, he said, "We thought the men might have been on drugs or intoxicated. Both had to be sedated to calm them down. One of the men still has not regained his right mind. They tell us that he sits in a corner pulling his legs up into his waist, saying, 'Call them off. Just call the dogs off!'"

UNDERSTANDING THE POWER IN JESUS'S NAME

If you have been a Christian for even for a short time, you have probably heard pastors and other believers frequently say, "There is power Jesus's name." Yet this truth never loses its strength, and it requires mentioning over and over again. The name of Jesus has power to save, power to deliver, and power to produce peace during times of trouble.

There are not enough words to accurately describe the wonder and authority that exist in the name of Jesus. Writing to the church at Philippi, the apostle Paul reminded the believers about the majesty of Jesus's name: *"Therefore God exalted him to the highest place and gave him the name that is above every name, that at the name of Jesus every knee should bow, in heaven and on earth and under the earth, and every tongue acknowledge that Jesus Christ is Lord, to the glory of God the Father"* (Philippians 2:9–11 NIV).

What awe-inspiring truth! The name of Jesus Christ is, and will forever remain, preeminent, surpassing every other name. His name reigns supreme above all names in both the seen and the unseen worlds and everything that is permitted to exist within them—including the spiritual forces that either wage war on behalf of God's beloved children or battle against them.

THE NAME OF JESUS HAS POWER TO SAVE, POWER TO DELIVER, AND POWER TO PRODUCE PEACE DURING TIMES OF TROUBLE.

"SAVIOR"

The first chapter of Matthew unveils the miracle of Jesus's birth, the power of His name, and His anointed calling as Savior.

Behold, the angel of the Lord appeared to him in a dream, saying, Joseph, you son of David, fear not to take to you Mary your wife: for that which is conceived in her is of the Holy Ghost. And she shall bring forth a son, and you shall call His name Jesus: for He shall save His people from their sins. (Matthew 1:20–21 KJVER)

In the natural world, most parents choose their children's names as a form of identity and to associate them with their families for the sake of lineage and heritage. These names are designations by which their offspring are known. Pastor Tony Evans gives these helpful insights into the significance of names:

> Names matter.
>
> When you say the name of a person, you are speaking of their identity. If you were to approach a group of people whom you know and ask to speak to someone named Avery, it would be Avery who answered. It wouldn't be Chris. The reason why Avery would answer is because that is his name. That is his identity. It is not Chris' identity.
>
> Names are more than nomenclature. Names involve identity. In the Bible, names were often given at the earliest possible time in an effort by the parents to define the hopes and dreams of their child. Thus, the parents would choose a name to reflect what the child was destined to become.[54]

In Jesus's case, He was not named by His earthly parents. His name was delivered to His father and mother by God the Father through the angel Gabriel, along with meaning of His name: "Savior."

> The name *Jesus*…means "Yahweh saves" or "Yahweh is salvation." Transliterated from Hebrew and Aramaic, the name is Yeshua. It is a combination of *Ya*, an abbreviation for *Yahweh*, the name of Israel's God (Exodus 3:14); and the verb *yasha*, meaning "rescue," "deliver," or "save."[55]

The apostle Peter declared, *"Salvation is found in no one else* [but Jesus Christ], *for there is no other name under heaven given to mankind by which we must be saved"* (Acts 4:12 NIV).

"GOD WITH US"

The passage in Matthew 1 about Jesus's birth also reveals that Jesus is *"God with us"*:

---

54. Tony Evans, *The Power of Jesus's Names* (Eugene, OR: Harvest House Publishers, 2019), 11.
55. "What Is the Meaning of the Name Jesus?" Got Questions, https://www.gotquestions.org/meaning-name-Jesus.html.

Now all this was done, that it might be fulfilled which was spoken of the Lord by the prophet, saying, Behold, a virgin shall be with child, and shall bring forth a Son, and they shall call His name Immanuel, which being interpreted is, God with us. (Matthew 1:22–23 KJVER)

When Christ came to earth, He brought God to us. In the Old Testament, God was generally considered to be mysterious and unapproachable, even though His ultimate desire was oneness with His people. He was somewhat elusive, although His presence was prominent when He manifested Himself. This distance between God and humankind caused by the fall was bridged through Jesus Christ. *"And the Word was made flesh, and dwelt among us, (and we beheld His glory, the glory as of the only begotten of the Father,) full of grace and truth"* (John 1:14 KJVER).

Our heavenly Father is revealed to us through Jesus, and, among His other attributes, He is our Redeemer. (See, for example, 1 Peter 1:18–19.) Jesus is "God with us" as the Reconciler and Savior who brought a resolution to the problem of sin, saving those who were separated from God. *"For if, while we were God's enemies, we were reconciled to him through the death of his Son, how much more, having been reconciled, shall we be saved through his life!"* (Romans 5:10 NIV).

As I have been emphasizing in this book, God comes to live within us through Jesus Christ when we are born again. Therefore, Jesus is not only God *with* us, but He is also God *in* us by the Spirit. All that He is comes to dwell in us. Our salvation in Christ gives us ongoing fellowship with the Father and enables us to live in a way that pleases Him. "My old self has been crucified with Christ. It is no longer I who live, but Christ lives in me. So I live in this earthly body by trusting in the Son of God, who loved me and gave himself for me" (Galatians 2:20 NLT).

POWER IN THE NAME OF JESUS

Even before His resurrection, Jesus explained to His disciples the heavenly resources and dynamic power available to Him: *"Don't you realize that I could ask my Father for thousands of angels to protect us, and he would send them instantly?"* (Matthew 26:53 NLT). After His resurrection, He told

His followers, *"All authority in heaven and on earth has been given to me"* (Matthew 28:18 NIV).

Jesus is Savior, He is "God with Us," and His power incorporates all the attributes listed in the Bible in relation to Him. For example, Isaiah 9:6 says, *"For to us a child is born, to us a son is given, and the government will be on his shoulders. And he will be called Wonderful Counselor, Mighty God, Everlasting Father, Prince of Peace"* (NIV). The name of Jesus, spoken from a believer's heart or mouth, is a call, an appeal, an invitation for Him to come in all His fullness! The mere mention of His name summons not only His presence but also the same Spirit that raised Him from the dead. Jesus's name—invited, welcomed, and celebrated—invokes resurrection power!

> The name "Jesus" is only powerful when connected with the risen Christ....
>
> "Jesus" is not a magic word given to Christians as a means of bringing trivial or ungodly matters to fruition.... When we use His name in power and miracles happen, *He* is glorified, not us. Christians are instructed to call on Jesus' name for protection, comfort, and in order to serve others.[56]

E. W. Kenyon, who was known for his great faith, declared, "Jesus has given you the right to use His name. That name can break the power of disease, the power of the adversary. That name can stop disease and failure from reigning over you. There is no disease that has ever come to man which this name cannot destroy."[57]

Martin Luther suffered greatly in his life and was rejected by many. Still, he believed that the name of Jesus had power, saying, "When I was abandoned by everybody, in my greatest weakness, trembling and afraid of death, when I was persecuted by this wicked world, then I often felt most surely the divine power in this name, Jesus Christ... So, by God's grace, I will live and die for that name."[58]

---

56. Candice Lucey, "Is There Power in the Name of Jesus?" Christianity.com, August 29, 2019, https://www.christianity.com/wiki/jesus-christ/is-there-power-in-the-name-of-jesus.html. Italics are in the original.
57. "E. W. Kenyon Quotes," Quotefancy, https://quotefancy.com/e-w-kenyon-quotes.
58. "Martin Luther Quotes," AZ Quotes, https://www.azquotes.com/quote/578104.

We all reach a point at some time in our lives when we are brought face-to-face with a human weakness or challenge that compels us to concede our utter powerlessness and vulnerability to fulfill God's purposes on our own. In John 15:5, Jesus said, *"Apart from me you can do nothing"* (NIV). Jesus means just that—without Him, we can do *nothing*. So, we are powerless without Jesus. But with Jesus, and in His name, we can do *all* things! (See, for example, Philippians 4:13.)

JESUS'S NAME—INVITED, WELCOMED, AND CELEBRATED—INVOKES RESURRECTION POWER!

PEACE IN THE NAME OF JESUS

Yet calling on the name of Jesus Christ is more than an appeal for His power. It is also a call for His peace because He is the Prince of Peace. Remember, the reason we are able to call on Jesus's name to destroy fear in our lives and bring us peace is that He is *"God with us"* (Matthew 1:23, various translations) *and in us* who defeated sin and death at the cross! Jesus Christ's name represents the unrestricted power, preservation, and authority of the triune God and all spiritual powers that stand ready to obey His commands.

The name of Jesus, invoked by a genuine, born-again believer, opens the heavens and summons heavenly agents. Demonic spirits are terrified when they find themselves face-to-face with these angelic hosts. Jesus's name will drive away the spirit of fear and every ungodly emotion associated with it. His name creates light, dispels darkness, and banishes anything that opposes our peace.

All that would stand between us and God's peace is subject to the power, majesty, and authority of Jesus's name! Proverbs 18:10 says, *"The name of the Lord is a fortified tower; the righteous run to it and are safe"* (NIV). And Psalm 46:1 says, *"God is our refuge and strength, an ever-present help in trouble*" (NIV). When we speak Jesus's name, all our fears—even those of sin, sickness, and death—lose their power.

JESUS'S NAME HAS ALL WE NEED

Always remember, while the people around you may not understand why you call on the name of Jesus, the spiritual world stands at attention every time you speak His name. Because you are a child of God, your voice carries with it the DNA of your heavenly Father. When you say the name of Jesus, the sound of your voice is a call to your Father to rescue and cover you.

As God's people call on the name of Jesus, the heavens are opened, and the powers of darkness are rebuked.

As born-again believers use the name of Jesus, His supernatural power is released to defeat anything that dares to threaten and terrorize us.

As Jesus's followers speak His name, the same Spirit who raised Him from the dead comes to our rescue! Consequently, frustration, depression, panic, and anxiety must go.

Because we are His children, our heavenly Father loves to save and deliver us from all that frightens us. We must never forget to call on Jesus's name for His salvation and deliverance! We don't even need to wait until we feel fearful. We must learn use His name every day, everywhere, in all circumstances. When we call on His name, it has all that we need.

12

PEACE THROUGH PRAYER

"As we pour out our bitterness, God pours in his peace."
—*F. B. Meyer*[59]

I'll pray for you" is a sentiment people often express as a type of courtesy to someone who is sick or has suffered the death of a loved one, although sometimes those words can feel empty to the one receiving them. Too often, we use the word *prayer* loosely.

Beyond the above form of expression, people often think of prayer as kneeling down to pray before going to bed, going up to the altar of a church to pray for a need, or asking for God's help on behalf of someone who has a prayer request. It is not uncommon to hear people talk about the feelings of peace and security they experience in such moments. Yet the peace they sense at those particular times is, unfortunately, often short-lived. Many people live somewhere in between peace and stress, or courage and fear,

---

59. "19 Beautiful Quotes About God's Peace," Christian Quotes, https://www.christianquotes.info/top-quotes/19-beautiful-quotes-about-gods-peace/.

because they don't understand what prayer really is and the transformation it can bring to their lives.

WHAT IS PRAYER?

The most basic misconception people have about prayer is that it consists of merely telling God what we want or need. Most people's prayers are more like a speech, with the conversation going in only one direction. But prayer can't be reduced to the act of a sender transmitting ideas to a receiver. It is not about one person doing all the talking but rather an ongoing *interaction* between God and an individual. Praying is two parties listening to one another and interacting; it is a dialogue and an interchange. Through prayer, we hear and then respond to the voice of God.

Theologian and philosopher Soren Kierkegaard said, "A man prayed, and at first he thought that prayer was talking. But he became more and more quiet until in the end he realized prayer is listening."[60] And François Fénelon expressed, "How can you expect God to speak in that gentle and inward voice which melts the soul, when you are making so much noise with your rapid reflections? Be silent and God will speak again."[61]

> **THROUGH PRAYER, WE HEAR AND THEN RESPOND TO THE VOICE OF GOD.**

In the Scriptures, prayer takes various forms, such as worship, lament, thanksgiving, confession, and petition—actions that create an environment in which God listens and acts. We can experience God's peace through prayer because prayer is a means of helping us work through our difficulties and trials, knowing that God hears our requests and will answer, even if His answers don't always come as fast as we would like them to. Here are several biblical examples of people who reached out to God during times of testing and received His help:

60. "Soren Kierkegaard Quotes," AZ Quotes, https://www.azquotes.com/quote/658234.
61. "François Fénelon Quotes," AZ Quotes, https://www.azquotes.com/quote/837741.

Jabez cried out to the God of Israel, "Oh, that you would bless me and enlarge my territory! Let your hand be with me, and keep me from harm so that I will be free from pain." And God granted his request.
(1 Chronicles 4:10 NIV)

[Shortly before His crucifixion, Jesus prayed,] *"Now my soul is troubled, and what shall I say? 'Father, save me from this hour'? No, it was for this very reason I came to this hour. Father, glorify your name!" Then a voice came from heaven, "I have glorified it, and will glorify it again."*
(John 12:27–28 NIV)

[The apostle Paul said,] *"Three times I pleaded with the Lord to take it [the thorn in his flesh] away from me. But he said to me, 'My grace is sufficient for you, for my power is made perfect in weakness.'"*
(2 Corinthians 12:8–9 NIV)

About midnight Paul and Silas were praying and singing hymns to God, and the other prisoners were listening to them. Suddenly there was such a violent earthquake that the foundations of the prison were shaken. At once all the prison doors flew open, and everyone's chains came loose.
(Acts 16:25–26 NIV)

Prayer calms the troubled waters of our lives, reminding us that God is with us in all circumstances.

Do not be anxious about anything, but in every situation, by prayer and petition, with thanksgiving, present your requests to God. And the peace of God, which transcends all understanding, will guard your hearts and your minds in Christ Jesus. (Philippians 4:6–7 NIV)

God doesn't want us to be overwhelmed with anxiety that is initiated by the intrusion of torturous thoughts caused by life's predicaments. When it appears that there is no immediate solution to a particular dilemma, we must choose between continuing to live in insufferable anxiety or receiving the peace that comes through surrendering the situation to the Lord.

When our distressed hearts wrestle with unsettling quandaries, it is time to turn to God through prayer, petition, and thanksgiving.

"One day Jesus was praying in a certain place. When he finished, one of his disciples said to him, 'Lord, teach us to pray...'" (Luke 11:1 NIV). *"Teach us to pray"* is a request we should all make of the Lord. The model prayer that Jesus taught to His disciples (and to us) is a series of communications addressed to our heavenly Father that include adoration, dedication, petition, intercession, and an appeal for protection, expressed with a heart of love and appreciation. While we are in prayer, God opens our eyes to see Him, and our whole being responds to Him with recognition and worship. Our prayers should be followed by thanksgiving for the revelations God gives us of His love, power, and care. As Paul wrote, *"By prayer and petition, with thanksgiving"* (Philippians 4:6 NIV).

PRAYING WITHOUT CEASING

Jesus believed in the necessity of continual prayer (see, for example, Luke 5:16; 6:12), and so should we. The apostle Paul's instructions to the believers in Thessalonica emphasized, *"**Pray without ceasing.** In every thing, give thanks: for this is the will of God in Christ Jesus concerning you. Quench not the Spirit"* (1 Thessalonians 5:17–19 KJV, KJVER). We are to pray without ceasing, be grateful, and not quench the Holy Spirit's ongoing work in our lives. In *My Utmost for His Highest*, Oswald Chambers wrote the following words in his unforgettable way:

> The voice of the Spirit of God is as gentle as a summer breeze—so gentle that unless you are living in complete fellowship and oneness with God, you will never hear it. The sense of warning and restraint that the Spirit gives comes to us in the most amazingly gentle ways. And if you are not sensitive enough to detect His voice, you will quench it, and your spiritual life will be impaired.[62]

If, in your fear, you resist God or turn away from Him, you will extinguish the fire of the Holy Spirit within you. But if you surrender to the

---

62. Oswald Chambers, *My Utmost for His Highest—Updated Edition*, ed. James Reimann (Grand Rapids, MI: Discovery House Publishers, 1992), August 13; see also https://utmost.org/do-not-quench-the-spirit/.

Lord, then God will raise you up from the painful and shameful places of your past and present, and you will walk in resurrection power. Jesus did not come to condemn us but to change us. (See John 3:17.) Now is the time to discover how to live a life of never-ending communication with the Father through an intimate relationship with the Holy Spirit.

Thomas Watson, an English minister who lived in the seventeenth century, wrote:

> [God] will give us peace in trouble. When there is a storm without, he will make music within. The world can create trouble in peace—but God can create peace in trouble. He will send the Comforter, who, as a dove, brings an olive-branch of peace in his mouth.[63]

NOW IS THE TIME TO DISCOVER HOW TO LIVE A LIFE OF NEVER-ENDING COMMUNICATION WITH THE FATHER THROUGH AN INTIMATE RELATIONSHIP WITH THE HOLY SPIRIT.

AN INTIMATE RELATIONSHIP WITH GOD'S SPIRIT

I had the honor of being raised by a father who understood the power of prayer and its correlation with peace. Again, I'm not talking about the kind of prayer we hear religious people perform in public places. I am talking about the type of prayer that travels with you in the private spaces of your daily life.

My dad was one of the happiest men I ever knew. In fact, people would often ask me, "Why is your father always so happy? Why is he always smiling and laughing?" The answer is that, early on in his Christian life, he was

63. Thomas Watson, *The Thomas Watson Collection: A Divine Cordial, The Ten Commandments, The Godly Man's Picture, The Lord's Prayer and Other Works* (Kyiv, Ukraine: Strelbytskyy Multimedia Publishing, 2021), https://books.google.com/books?id=TCgzEAAAQBAJ&pg=PT315&lpg=PT315&dq=The+world+can+create+trouble+in+peace,+but+God+can+create+peace+in+trouble+(Thomas+Watson).

blessed to enter into an intimate relationship with God that became the source of his peace, strength, and courage in the midst of all of the challenges he faced over the years.

My dad wasn't perfect, but his prayer life was as close to perfection as any I have ever seen. He didn't just pray in church, at special prayer gatherings, or at holiday meals. He prayed every day, in all places, at all times. He truly lived in God's presence. I believe that the quality of his prayer life was the reason for his gentle demeanor and peaceful disposition, as well as the sense of security I felt when I was around him.

I never saw anyone pray quite like my dad prayed. The first time I noticed his unique prayer life was when I was still rather young, and we drove to the grocery store to buy bread and milk. When we walked through the grocery store, I heard my father pray, "Lord, what kind of bread shall we get today? Brown bread or white?" At first, I thought he was kidding me or performing to make me laugh, but he wasn't. As I followed him around the store, it was as if he were in constant contact with the Lord, except for those moments when he turned to briefly address me, saying, "Marky, do we need anything else at home? How about lunch meat?" or "Are we out of mustard?" After I answered him, he would return to what he was doing and continue his conversation with God, saying, for example, "Father, thank You for Your goodness! Thank You for Your grace and Your unmerited favor."

Other times, I thought he was talking to himself, but he was actually having a conversation with the Lord. Every so often, I would hear him pray, as if out of nowhere, something like, "Father, thank You for giving me the answer to fixing the motor in our car!" As soon as he made these brief prayers, he would break out into song. And I can remember him whistling hymns or gospel tunes on a thousand car rides to and from school or while we were working together at the house.

In addition, I watched my father pray in the most unusual places at some of the most notable times. I remember when I went with him to drop trash into a deep landfill. As Dad prepared to back our old pickup truck to the edge of the landfill, which was about a hundred and fifty feet deep, I heard him say, "Thank You, Lord, for keeping Your hand on Marky and me!"

Few people know that I worked with my dad as a welder's assistant when I was eighteen. One specific assignment required our stretching high-powered welding cables up, over, and into a giant sand pit. Then we both had to descend into the large container to repair metal that had been damaged over the years from having sand and rock dispensed from it. It was a dangerous job, yet not one time did I ever hear my father express fear or worry about what might happen to us. We simply prayed, asking God to bless our day and giving thanks for our jobs as welders and repairers!

Thus, my father not only walked in peace, but he also worked in peace. The mysterious power that emboldened him to be continually fear-free and happily content came from his praying without ceasing. His lifestyle of prayer was something I came to truly appreciate only many years later when I had my first son, Jake, and I began to pray for his well-being and protection too. And I am grateful that, as the years passed, and my father grew older, his amazing inner light never went out. Even after my mother passed, which was one of the most challenging times he ever had to endure, he remained the happiest man I had ever met. Even after learning he had Parkinson's disease, my father never lost his peace, joy, or energy. He remained courageous throughout his life. I have often said that my dad seemed to have more peace and joy in his eighties than most people have in their twenties!

LIVING CONTINUALLY IN PEACE

I have shared about my father's prayer life to illustrate the possibilities of living in continual peace and freedom from fear through a relationship with the heavenly Father in which you communicate with Him moment by moment. You can have a relationship with your Father twenty-four hours a day, seven days a week. Is such an ongoing relationship with God really possible? Yes, and you can really have it! Be radical in your prayers and enthusiastic about your connection with God in both your private life and your public life. As you live this radical lifestyle, some people might think you've lost your mind, but just keep praying to your heavenly Father, who guarantees you lasting peace of mind through Jesus. (See John 14:27.)

If your relationship with God consists of only "touching base" with Him sporadically, or if you have been treating God like a stranger, you have chosen the wrong path, and your peace of mind will suffer. You won't be able to experience consistent peace until you learn to walk in constant connection with the Father.

You must no longer ignore the God who lives within you. Choose to invite the Holy Spirit to accompany you every moment of the day, and then treat Him as if He *is* with you every moment of the day, because He is! Instead of speaking about your worries or complaints, enjoy conversing with the Holy Spirit. And don't be surprised when He begins to respond. He has been waiting for you to stumble onto this secret of passionate prayer. When you awake in the morning, greet Him. As you are getting ready for your day, speak with Him and listen for His direction. When you get in your car, quiet your spirit, enjoy His presence, and seek to hear His voice. When you are at your job, consult with Him before you consult with others. You will be amazed at how many doors of opportunity will begin to open for you. It's not "magic"—it's His continual presence in your life.

CHOOSE TO INVITE THE HOLY SPIRIT TO ACCOMPANY YOU EVERY MOMENT OF THE DAY, AND THEN TREAT HIM AS IF HE IS WITH YOU EVERY MOMENT OF THE DAY, BECAUSE HE IS!

If you genuinely desire a fear-free life full of peace, make a covenant with the Lord right now that you will cease praying to Him "religiously" and instead pray passionately and continually in His presence. If you are willing to make that commitment, your entire life will noticeably shift. It has been said that it takes thirty days to create a new habit and ninety days to break an old habit. I encourage you to invite Jesus into your daily thoughts and to pursue conversations with God. As you do, the reality of His constant presence in your life will become evident to you, and you will never want to turn back to your old way of living. You will be living a fear-free life.

13

ENFORCING PEACE

"We know that peace is the condition under which mankind
was meant to flourish. Yet peace does not exist of its own will.
It depends on us, on our courage to build it and guard it
and pass it on to future generations."
—*President Ronald Reagan*[64]

Sometimes we think that once we receive peace from God, our peace
will never be challenged again. We are surprised and confused when our
peace starts to slip away, not realizing that receiving and maintaining peace
often requires spiritual force. Peace must be pursued purposefully and
steadfastly.

A THREAT TO PEACE

Many people today are not familiar with the "duck and cover" nuclear
bomb drills for children that were conducted in America's public schools
in the 1950s and 60s, such as the exercises I participated in when I was a
little boy. I remember them all too well. These were drills in which children

---

64. Ronald Reagan, "Address to the Nation on National Security," February 26, 1986,
https://www.reaganlibrary.gov/archives/speech/address-nation-national-security.

were trained to respond to a possible military attack against our country by the Soviet Union. My classmates and I knew the test was beginning when we heard the sound of sirens followed by instructions from our teachers to place our pencils and papers neatly in front of us and get under our desks, where we were to hunker down for cover as quickly as possible.

As you can imagine, such exercises were rather terrifying for children of that day—at least, at first. Like most things kids experience regularly, after a couple of years, they grew accustomed to them, especially as teachers and parents assured them that the possibility of something so horrible occurring in their lifetime was very remote.

Such was the case in my community. Well, that is, until one morning in October 1962 when all the students in our elementary school were suddenly ushered out of their classrooms by fear-stricken teachers who were working hard not to reveal their panic in front of their young pupils. I was only five-and-a-half years old on the day our class was abruptly cut short. Our teacher carefully escorted the class to the front of the school, where our parents would be picking us up to take us home.

This time, there was a real chance that our nation might be under the threat of nuclear war. Although I was too young at the time to understand the ramifications of such a potentially catastrophic event, I would later discover just how close we were to having everything we had trained to protect ourselves against become a reality.

In 1960, Soviet leader Nikita Khrushchev had determined to place missiles armed with nuclear warheads on the coast of Cuba that had the capacity to reach targets in the United States. In the summer of 1962, Khrushchev began to ship ballistic missiles to Cuba, along with technicians to operate them. He believed that President John F. Kennedy was weak and would not react to the Soviet move. In October 1962, when Kennedy learned that the Soviets and Cubans were preparing to make the missiles operational, a thirteen-day confrontation between America and the Soviet Union commenced that nearly initiated a full-on nuclear war. I remember the trembling in my parents' voices that October day as they drove me home from school, talking about the possibility of our family being under the threat of a nuclear attack.

Kennedy, after extensive consultation with his foreign policy and military advisers, "quarantined," or blockaded, Cuba beginning on October 22, 1962. The two sides stood on the brink of nuclear war, but Khrushchev eventually capitulated and dismantled the missiles. I believe it required magnificent courage for Kennedy to remain resolute in resolving the crisis and turning back the Soviet threat.[65]

The Cuban Missile Crisis has become a matter of great debate among historians and politicians over the years. Some historians believe the situation was resolved by mutual agreements that secured the Americans' safety within those fragile hours, sending the Soviets into retreat. However, I think that one hard fact remains: it was not discussions of compromise that ultimately kept the Soviet Union from firing those deadly weapons of mass destruction on our nation. While it's true that Kennedy brilliantly communicated with America's aggressors concerning the withdrawal of the weapons, it was not his words that changed their minds. It was his courageous resolve to, if necessary, unleash the full power of our military upon the Soviets.

According to most historians, the Cuban Missile Crisis was one of the most defining moments in the history of America's national security. While it was a tense moment in the nation's history, it was also a defining moment for President Kennedy, who demonstrated faith, courage, and resolve in responding to the threat. On September 13, Kennedy had warned, "If at any time the Communist build-up in Cuba were to endanger or interfere with our security in any way…or if Cuba should ever…become an offensive military base of significant capacity for the Soviet Union, then this country will do whatever must be done to protect its own security and that of its allies."[66]

---

65. The Editors of Encyclopaedia Britannica, "Cuban Missile Crisis," Britannica, https://www.britannica.com/event/Cuban-missile-crisis; Patrick J. Kiger, "Key Moments in the Cuban Missile Crisis," June 17, 2019, History, https://www.history.com/news/cuban-missile-crisis-timeline-jfk-khrushchev.
66. "Forty Years Ago: The Cuban Missile Crisis," *Prologue Magazine*, Fall 2002, vol. 34, no. 3, https://www.archives.gov/publications/prologue/2002/fall/cuban-missiles.html.

A LESSON IN PEACE

We can draw a significant lesson about overcoming fear from the example of Kennedy's resolve. He refused to be bullied by an aggressor nation but was willing to maintain peace through force. Likewise, peace in our lives is both secured and preserved through God's power as we determine not to allow the enemy to bully us into fear.

As previously mentioned, if you ask the average person why they are fearful, they will likely point to different types of narratives that led them to fear instead of pointing to the mastermind behind it all: our spiritual enemy, Satan. But unless we learn to discern our enemy and rely on God's power, we will continue to be deceived and terrorized by the devil's fear tactics.

When fear takes hold of us, it is as if we duck under our metaphorical desks seeking protection from a force we think may overwhelm us. We must realize that our invisible diabolical enemy has *already* been defeated. *"When He [Jesus] had disarmed the rulers and authorities, He made a public display of them, having triumphed over them through Him"* (Colossians 2:15 NASB). Jesus reigns as the triumphant King, and we participate in His glorious victory over the enemy.

PEACE IS BOTH SECURED AND PRESERVED THROUGH GOD'S POWER.

THE SUPERPOWER OF PEACE

God's peace is predicated on our intimate, personal relationship with the Holy Spirit, who resides in us and enables us to live victoriously. The Spirit's power produces peace, faith, provision, security, courage, tenacity, and perseverance—no matter what is happening around us.

In 2007, the Lord placed a word in Jordana's spirit that we didn't completely understand at the time because it was before the Wall Street meltdown and the housing crisis that began shortly afterward, and it was well before the many challenges we are currently facing. Little did we know that, within a matter of months, we would soon gain a clearer understanding of this word. God's message was simple but prophetically profound: "Dangerous is the man or woman who finds peace in this season, for there is power in peace."

As the Holy Spirit began to reveal what lay ahead, it soon became apparent that He was forewarning us of an hour when peace would become a rare commodity—but it would be a superpower for those who possessed it. In the following years, like many others, we were forced to face incredible challenges. But because of the word we had received, we remembered to trust and rely on God; we sought to enter into His peace and remain in it.

The third chapter of Proverbs declares a powerful word for our times: *"Trust in the LORD with all your heart and lean not on your own understanding; in all your ways submit to him, and he will make your paths straight"* (Proverbs 3:5–6 NIV). I love this passage because it reminds me that our peace is based on the creative power of God's supernatural presence. In times like these, He makes our paths straight. He makes a way where there seems to be no way!

"DANGEROUS IS THE MAN OR WOMAN WHO FINDS PEACE IN THIS SEASON, FOR THERE IS POWER IN PEACE."

"GREAT PEACE"

As long as there is evil in this world, your peace will be threatened. Again, that peace must be maintained through spiritual strength and resolve. The only thing that intimidates and drives back Satan is power. The devil does not fear those who are faithless toward Christ, and he does not respect cowardice or weakness. He is a ruthless terrorist and killer whose demonic cohorts are committed to threatening and frightening anyone who is not prepared to stand up and resist them. That is why he targets the unfaithful, the insecure, and the weak.

Like a large cat that captures and toys with its prey, Satan enjoys play-ing with the innocent and defenseless. In 1 Peter 5:8, we are given this warning by the apostle Peter: *"Be self-controlled and alert. Your enemy the devil prowls around like a roaring lion looking for someone to devour"* (NIV84). *"Be self-controlled and alert"*! These are the warning cries of a shepherd call-ing his sheep to be watchful against the subtle designs of a malevolent lion prowling around the flock in the darkness. We must heed this warning to be watchful against Satan's stealthy attempts to attack us and steal our peace.

Sometimes the devil disguises himself an *"angel of light"* (see 2 Corinthians 11:14, various translations) in order to deceive us; but, underneath, he is still like the fierce king of the jungle that, by its terrible roar, seeks to intimidate its potential prey. Nevertheless, that fierce lion can be rendered powerless by the trifecta of faith, God's Word, and super-natural peace! He is terrorized by the faith of God's people who carry the power of God's Word and refuse to evacuate their God-given peace.

"Great peace have those who love your law, and nothing can make them stumble" (Psalm 119:165 NIV). Our faith feeds on the Word of God, which brings us peace as we receive and obey it. Though we might be persecuted and go through forbidding times, we can have even *"great peace"* under those circumstances. As we remain in our Father's presence, we have the power of His Word and the energy of His comforting Spirit, who gives us hope. We stand in that energizing spiritual power against the bully-ing spirits of fear that are sweeping our nation and the world, and we are ready to engage in spiritual warfare, if necessary, to defend what we know is rightfully ours in Jesus's name.

In Deuteronomy 20, we are reminded that even when we face the most formidable challenges of our lives, we do not have to fear what may come because we are not alone. God is with us!

When you go to war against your enemies and see horses and chariots and an army greater than yours, do not be afraid of them, because the Lord your God, who brought you up out of Egypt, will be with you. When you are about to go into battle, the priest shall come forward and address the army. He shall say: "Hear, Israel: Today you are going into battle against your enemies. Do not be fainthearted or afraid; do

*not panic or be terrified by them. For the Lord your God is the one
who goes with you to fight for you against your enemies to give you
victory."* (Deuteronomy 20:1–4 NIV)

David acknowledged being afraid when he fled from Saul and entered
the land of Israel's enemies, the Philistines. But when he was afraid, he put
his trust in the Lord:

*My enemies have trampled upon me all day long, for they are
many who fight proudly against me. When I am afraid, I will put
my trust in You. In God, whose word I praise, in God I have put
my trust; I shall not be afraid. What can mere mortals do to me?*
(Psalm 56:2–4 NASB)

In Psalm 34, David praised God for delivering him from the Philistines
and from all his fears:

*I sought the LORD, and he answered me; he delivered me from all my
fears. Those who look to him are radiant; their faces are never covered
with shame. This poor man called, and the LORD heard him; he saved
him out of all his troubles. The angel of the LORD encamps around
those who fear him, and he delivers them.* (Psalm 34:4–7 NIV)

When life's skirmishes and battles come our way—when our peace is
under attack and we realize that living for Christ does not buffer us from
all struggles, criticisms, and conflicts—we can trust in the Lord and rest in
His Word, and His peace will abundantly fill us.

"PERFECT PEACE"

God is faithful to watch over us, no matter what fears we face. *"Thou
wilt keep him in perfect peace, whose mind is stayed on thee: because he trusteth
in thee"* (Isaiah 26:3 KJV). In his commentary on Isaiah 26:3, Alfred Barnes
interpreted two key phrases from this verse:

In perfect peace – Hebrew as in the Margin, "Peace, peace;" the
repetition of the word denoting, as is usual in Hebrew, emphasis,
and here evidently meaning undisturbed, perfect peace. That is,
the mind that has confidence in God shall not be agitated by the

trials to which it shall be subject; by persecution, poverty, sickness, want, or bereavement....

Whose mind is stayed on thee –... The word which is rendered "mind"...is derived from...yâtsar *to form, create, devise;* and it properly denotes that which is formed or made (Psalm 103:14; Isaiah 29:16; Hebrews 2:18). Then it denotes anything that is formed by the mind—its thoughts, imaginations, devices (Genesis 8:21; Deuteronomy 31:21). Here it may mean the thoughts themselves, or the mind that forms the thoughts.... The expression, "is stayed on thee," in the Hebrew does not express the idea that the mind is stayed on God, though that is evidently implied. The Hebrew is simply, whose mind is stayed, supported...; that is, evidently, supported by God. There is no other support but that; and the connection requires us to understand this of him."[67]

God has given us the supernatural ability to discern, drive back, and defeat unauthorized spirits of fear so we can live in His perfect peace. Spirit-filled Christians carry the authority to expose and expel these demonic peace-thieves! The most dangerous demon is the one we have not yet discerned, the one that tries to infuse our thoughts with subtle deception and confusion. Through God's Word and the leading of the Spirit, let us reject the enemy's deceit and disorder; instead, let us accept the truth and peace of the Prince of Peace, who will liberate us from fear and empower us to resist the enemy.

Yes, Satan is a ruthless bully and killer who preys upon ignorance and seeks to kill our peace. However, our weapons of warfare are powerful to bring down the enemy. "*For the weapons of our warfare are not of the flesh, but divinely powerful for the destruction of fortresses. We are destroying arguments and all arrogance raised against the knowledge of God, and we are taking every thought captive to the obedience of Christ*" (2 Corinthians 10:4–5 NASB). Therefore, let us "*be strong in the Lord and in the strength of His might*" (Ephesians 6:10 NASB).

---

67. "Barnes's Isaiah 26:3 Bible Commentary," Godtube, https://www.godtube.com/bible/isaiah/26-3. Light edits have been made for consistency of style with this book.

> *GOD HAS GIVEN US THE SUPERNATURAL ABILITY*
> *TO DISCERN, DRIVE BACK, AND DEFEAT UNAUTHORIZED*
> *SPIRITS OF FEAR SO WE CAN LIVE IN HIS PERFECT PEACE.*

THE STIRRING OF GOD

As we look to the Lord in difficult and fearful times, He will stir our spirits to take courage and continue to do His will. The following are several biblical examples of this.

> *Now in the first year of Cyrus king of Persia, in order to fulfill the word of the Lord by the mouth of Jeremiah, the Lord stirred up the spirit of Cyrus king of Persia.... Then the heads of fathers' households of Judah and Benjamin and the priests and the Levites rose up, everyone **whose spirit God had stirred to go up to rebuild the house of the Lord** which is in Jerusalem.* (Ezra 1:1, 5 NASB)

The Lord God stirred up the king of Persia to help the Israelites who were living in exile in his kingdom. He also stirred the spirits of leaders, priests, and Levites among His people to go back to Jerusalem to work on rebuilding the temple. People who had been in exile for decades experienced a divine, forceful, and successful stirring in their spirits. This stirring was necessary to counteract any despair, discouragement, or aversion to traveling such a long distance to rebuild God's house that they may have had.

> *So the woman gave birth to a son and named him Samson; and the child grew up and the Lord blessed him. And **the Spirit of the Lord began to stir him....*** (Judges 13:24–25 NASB)

In Judges 13:25, the Hebrew word translated *"stir"* is *paam*, whose meanings include "to thrust," "to impel," or "to stir."[68] In those times when we are complacent, paralyzed by anxiety, or simply in need of moving

---

68. *NAS Exhaustive Concordance*, Bible Hub, https://biblehub.com/hebrew/6470.htm.

forward in God's purposes, the Spirit stirs us to action. Being stirred is a divine intervention deep in our souls where we feel strongly impressed and empowered to proceed in a faith generated by the breath of God. When the Creator stimulates and propels us toward action, it is a reminder to us that we are not alone; when we are afraid or have lost hope, the hand of God continues to touch and move us.

> *Wherefore I put you in remembrance that you stir up the gift of God, which is in you by the putting on of my hands.* (2 Timothy 1:6 KJVER)

"Stir up the gift of God, which is in you." The Greek word translated *"stir up"* means "to kindle afresh," "stir up the fire," and "fan the flame of."[69] The *New International Version* and other translations render the above phrase as *"fan into flame the gift of God."* The *New American Standard Bible* renders it as *"kindle afresh the gift of God,"* and other translations use similar wording, such as "rekindle."

Right after Paul reminded Timothy to *"stir up"* or *"fan into flame"* the spiritual gift God had given him, the apostle wrote, *"For God has not given us the spirit of fear; but of power, and of love, and of a sound mind ["self-discipline,"* various translations]" (2 Timothy 1:7 KJVER). The spirit that God has given us is not a spirit of fear or cowardice. Rather, we have received a spirit of power and love, a spirit that enables us to discipline ourselves.

We have more power within us than we imagine! When our spiritual lives have cooled down due to a weakened devotion to God, a loss of confidence, life's disappointments, or failure, the Holy Spirit operates within us, stirring us up again with divine passion. However, "fanning into flame" requires our human spirits to cooperate with the Holy Spirit who is stirring us up; we must move our spirits to urge our souls to faith and action. Remember, we have the potential to either quench the Spirit's gifts or to fan them into flame. We fan the flames by continuing to *"keep in step with the Spirit"* (Galatians 5:25 NIV, ESV). As the *New Living Translation* puts it, *"Since we are living by the Spirit, let us follow the Spirit's leading in every part of our lives"* (Galatians 5:25).

---

69. *Strong's Concordance* and *NAS Exhaustive Concordance*, Bible Hub, https://biblehub.com/greek/329.htm.

RECLAIMING OUR PEACE

Make no mistake about it: an unparalleled outpouring of the Holy Spirit has begun. Revival is not "coming"—it is already upon us! There is no doubt in my mind that a powerful anointing is returning to the church—to God's people, to you and me—to reclaim our God-given peace through the force of faith that quietly resides within us just beneath the surface of our souls. No longer will we allow the devil's threats to make us retreat into a fetal position or send us running for cover. No longer will we crawl under our excuses or hunker down and hide our heads. We are warriors and champions. (See, for example, Romans 8:37.) We are kings and priests to our God. (See, for example, Revelation 5:10). We are God's own children. (See, for example, 1 John 3:1.) We are men and women of spiritual warfare, trained to fight in the army of the Lord! (See, for example, Ephesians 6:10–18.) Fear must not win!

I can hear the voice of King David shouting:

Lift up your gates, ye princes, and be ye lifted up, ye everlasting doors; and the king of glory shall come in. Who is this king of glory? the Lord strong and mighty, the Lord mighty in battle. Lift up your gates, ye princes; and be ye lift up, ye everlasting doors; and the king of glory shall come in. Who is this king of glory? The Lord of hosts, he is this king of glory. (Psalm 24:7–10 bst)

Let us remember that when we live in a state of peace during difficult times, we are spiritually "dangerous" because there's power in peace as it guards our hearts and minds in Christ (see Philippians 4:7) and enables us to keep moving forward in God's purposes. Let us stir up the gifts God has given us, not giving in to fear or timidity but courageously preserving Christ's peace in our hearts as we continue to build His kingdom on earth.

14

LIVING FREE OF FEAR

*"A born-again person ought to possess
unspeakable peace in the spirit."
—Watchman Nee*[70]

In this book—through stories, illustrations, and biblical truths—we have identified the primary source of fear, circumstances that lead to anxiety and dread in our lives, and powerful principles for addressing our fears so we can live fear-free lives. In this chapter, I want to focus on ten main principles for living free of fear that we have covered to this point so you can keep them at the forefront of your thoughts as you address the specific fears and anxieties in your life. Then, in chapter 15, we will discuss one last but essential principle for overcoming fear.

Remember, while the world continually offers us plenty of reasons to return to the status quo of living with fear, we do not have to settle for that way of life. The fear-free life is available to all who choose it! The following words of King David show us how to open the door to a purposeful and peaceful life. We don't know for certain which fears ran through David's mind when he wrote Psalm 139, but he was clearly troubled when he

---

70. "Watchman Nee Quote," LibQuotes, https://libquotes.com/watchman-nee/quote/lbn9z2j.

expressed, *"Search me, God, and know my heart; test me and know my anxious thoughts"* (Psalm 139:23 NIV).

Perhaps David was worried about his safety or his future. (See verses 19–21.) However, David recognized that God could see the depths of his anxieties and fears. He wanted to share his worst fears with the Lord so he could face them and be free of them. We can do the same. What we fear the most often reveals the area in which we trust God the least. But when we recognize and admit our fears, we can begin to trust God with them.

As I expressed earlier, the principles for fear-free living in this book can be applied to any fear that you feel is holding you prisoner. But there's a catch: you have to *use* them! Once you know these principles, it's up to you to apply them so you can access the God-given abilities, purposes, joy, health, and peace that are rightfully yours.

Some of the following principles overlap with one another, but all are significant to review and apply individually.

PRINCIPLES FOR FEAR-FREE LIVING

PRINCIPLE 1: STAY IN GOD'S PRESENCE

Gaining victory over any type of fear in our lives begins with our acknowledging and living in the presence of the Father. It is essential that we be mindful of God's presence in our lives every moment of the day. As we experience His *manifest* presence—or as we recognize His *omnipresence*, whether we sense Him or not—we can live in peace, joy, and victory, knowing that our heavenly Father never leaves or forsakes us. (See Deuteronomy 31:6.)

Regardless of what difficulties we experience in life, God will sustain us. Though we may not feel courageous, we *can* stand up against our fears, knowing that our Father stands before us, beside us, and behind us. God is on our side. He is greater than any of our problems. Remember, the giants of this world pale in comparison to His splendor. In His presence, problems shrink, and fears dissipate.

"'For in him [God] *we live and move and have our being.' As some of your own poets have said, 'We are his offspring'"* (Acts 17:28 NIV). Perhaps

no words can better express our constant dependence on God than these. God is the fountain of life, and He upholds you each moment. Your very life and being, and every movement you make, is proof that God is with you—enlivening you with His own life, upholding you by His power, and sustaining you by His love.

PRINCIPLE 2: FOLLOW THE FATHER'S INSTRUCTIONS

God's instructions for living, given through His Word, are creative, and they carry the supernatural ability to teach, rebuke, correct, and restore us. *"All Scripture is God-breathed and is useful for teaching, rebuking, correcting and training in righteousness, so that the servant of God may be thoroughly equipped for every good work"* (2 Timothy 3:16–17 NIV).

Our heavenly Father's instructions safeguard and maintain us. They produce faith in us that can conquer fear. Anxiety and intimidation hold no power over those who walk according to God's revealed Word. His instructions have heaven's backing and the Holy Spirit's power. Through the Word, we have the assurance of God's presence and the peace of Christ in our lives.

It's important to speak God's Word aloud, reminding ourselves verbally of who He is and declaring His promises. Whenever we sense the ungoverned emotion or unnatural spirit of fear working to paralyze us, we must remember the power we have to rebuke and refute the evil one by quoting our Father's promises for our lives and futures.

PRINCIPLE 3: HAVE FAITH (THE GOD KIND)

Years ago, my brother, Chuck, came home from Bible college and shared with me an illustration he had heard from one of his professors. This is how it went: A student asked his master, "What is faith?" The teacher directed his student to a deep, treacherous canyon with a tightwire stretched across it from one side to the other. He then asked his student to bring him a wheelbarrow. When the student returned with the wheelbarrow, the teacher asked him to follow him to the edge of the cliff where the tightwire was secured. He then asked his student, "Do you know what *true* faith is?" The student, supposing he had discovered the answer, quickly replied, "I've got it! It is like me taking this wheelbarrow and carefully pushing it across this tightwire to the other side of this deep canyon." The teacher smiled and replied, "No, true faith is for you to get in the wheelbarrow and allow *me* to push *you* across the tightwire to the other side of this deep canyon."

I am sure that this story—and variations of it—has been shared many times over the years, but I've never forgotten it. You see, discovering, experiencing, and even enjoying a fear-free life require far more than trusting God to give us the courage to stay in control. Living a life without fear means having the faith and courage to *release* all our power and turn it over to the hands of the One who possesses the balance and ability to carry us across all the tightwires of life.

Such faith originates with God. Most Bible versions translate Mark 11:22 as *"Have faith in God,"* but that's not what it says in the original Greek. *Young's Literal Translation* renders the phrase as *"Have faith of God."* In the *Worrell New Testament*, this verse reads, *"Have the faith of God."* Those who have genuine faith have God's own faith. By having "the God kind of faith," we have genuine faith in the Lord, not something fabricated, so we are able to trust Him with all our concerns. When we have confidence, courage, and faith in God's power, it will chase away all fears that would dare to oppose us.

PRINCIPLE 4: DECIDE TO BELIEVE GOD

"What you decide on will be done, and light will shine on your ways" (Job 22:28 NIV). When you make the right decisions—according to God's Word and from a place of faith, not fear—what you decide will not be frustrated but will be achieved and ratified by God. The Lord will illuminate your path, giving you comfort and success in all your counsels, courses, and actions. No longer will you live in a land of darkness, doubt, and confusion.

You must make up your mind now that you believe God's Word concerning His power to protect and preserve you. You cannot be double-minded, fluctuating between a prison of fear and the peace of God. A fear-free life requires being resolute, determined to be led by the Spirit and not held hostage between two opposing belief systems. As darkness and light cannot coexist in the same place, fear and faith are incompatible and cannot occupy the same space.

Martin Luther King Jr. said, "Darkness cannot drive out darkness, only light can do that."[71] The Word of God acts like a light switch; if you turn it on by reading and applying it, the darkness disappears in a flash of light. Then you can bask in the sunshine of God's presence. But this does require you to make a decision. Where do you prefer to live: in the light whose source is Christ or in the darkness caused by fear?

YOU MUST MAKE UP YOUR MIND NOW THAT YOU BELIEVE GOD'S WORD CONCERNING HIS POWER TO PROTECT AND PRESERVE YOU.

Choosing to live in a secure place of peace is the best decision you could make, but it is the road less traveled. It requires the kind of faith that stands against all fears that question or oppose God's Word and power. Elijah, the Old Testament prophet and champion of faith, challenged the Israelites who were following the false god Baal by saying, *"How long halt* ["*hesitate*" AMP] *you between two opinions? if the Lord be God, follow Him"* (1 Kings 18:21 KJVER). Among the meanings of the Hebrew word translated *"halt"* or *"hesitate"* is "become lame,"[72] and one of the senses of the Hebrew word rendered *"opinion"* is "divided (in mind)."[73]

Elijah's challenge to the people was the same as it is to us today: "Believe God entirely or not at all. You cannot doubt God and have faith in Him at the same time." Again, the key here is to choose faith over fear.

I find it interesting that Elijah's challenge left the Israelites speechless. Verse 21 concludes, *"And the people answered him not a word"* (KJV, KJVER). This is what indecisiveness does—it puts you in a comatose-like state in which you do not respond to God's promises or live life to the fullest. You're frozen, paralyzed, stuck in limbo.

In contrast, faith is initiated by a solid decision to believe, trust, and rely on God's power, which bolsters you to rise up, stand up, and fight for

---

71. "Quotations," Martin Luther King, Jr. Memorial, National Parks Service, https://www.nps.gov/mlkm/learn/quotations.htm.
72. *Strong's*, #6452, https://biblehub.com/hebrew/6452.htm.
73. *Strong's*, #5587, https://biblehub.com/hebrew/5587.htm.

your life to the absolute fullest with no fear of pain or opposition. Faith grants you access to supernatural power, so that you can replace worry with confidence. Then you can say, as King David did:

> *Let them now that fear the LORD say, that His mercy endures for ever. I called upon the LORD in distress: the LORD answered me, and set me in a large place. The LORD is on my side; I will not fear: what can man do to me? The LORD takes my part with them that help me: therefore shall I see my desire upon them that hate me. It is better to trust in the LORD than to put confidence in man. It is better to trust in the LORD than to put confidence in princes..... The LORD is my strength and song, and is become my salvation. The voice of rejoicing and salvation is in the tabernacles of the righteous: the right hand of the LORD does valiantly. The right hand of the LORD is exalted: the right hand of the LORD does valiantly. I shall not die, but live, and declare the works of the LORD.*
> (Psalm 118:4–9, 14–17 KJVER)

PRINCIPLE 5: TRUST IN THE LORD

From God alone comes true prosperity, and He knows the way to fulfilling His purposes. He knows what benefits us, and He can free us from the fear that restrains us from receiving all that He has for us. Therefore, it is wise for us to place our trust wholly in Him rather than in our own judgment.

RELEASING OUR FEARS TO GOD

> *Trust in and rely confidently on the Lord with all your heart and do not rely on your own insight or understanding. In all your ways know and acknowledge and recognize Him, and He will make your paths straight and smooth [removing obstacles that block your way].*
> (Proverbs 3:5–6 AMP)

The Hebrew term for *"trust"* in this passage is *bâṭach*, which means "to trust," "to have confidence," "to be bold," and "to be secure."[74] When we place our trust in God, our worries and fears will be released from us.

---

74. *Old Testament Hebrew Lexical Dictionary* (*Strong's*, #982), https://www.studylight.org/lexicons/eng/hebrew/982.html.

I like to use the imagery of a balloon when teaching sessions on finding freedom from fear. I ask the attendees to close their eyes and think about their deepest concerns. Then, I ask them to imagine allowing the Holy Spirit to breathe out their worries into a hot-air balloon. Finally, I ask them to envision the release of that balloon. The power of God lifts the balloon, and it ascends—with all their cares and worries—drifting upwards, floating away out of sight until their anxieties have disappeared from their thoughts.

This is precisely what God does for those who dare to release their burdens and anxieties to Him. Trusting God means more than standing and believing something; it means releasing what hinders us! Let it go, cast it off, and discharge it, giving it to the Lord forever. "[Cast] *all your cares [all your anxieties, all your worries, and all your concerns, once and for all] on Him, for He cares about you [with deepest affection, and watches over you very carefully]*" (1 Peter 5:7 AMP).

LEANING ON GOD'S UNDERSTANDING

When you place your trust in the God of all creation—the God who lives within you—He will also clear a path before you. He stands within you not necessarily to meet every opposition but to create a way for the power of His plan and purpose residing within you to manifest!

From our human standpoint, with its limited perception, we see only part of the picture God is painting of our lives. If we are going to trust Him completely, we have to let go of our pride, programs, and plans. Even our best-laid plans cannot begin to approach the magnificent wisdom of God's plan. "*For the foolishness of God is wiser than human wisdom*" (1 Corinthians 1:25 NIV). Speaking through the prophet Isaiah, God said, "*For as the heavens are higher than the earth, so are My ways higher than your ways, and My thoughts than your thoughts*" (Isaiah 55:9 NKJV).

Our human understanding can quickly get us in trouble because we are easily led astray. What appears correct could very well be wrong because we have a narrow view, producing a distorted perception. If we desire a sure, straight path, we must not lean on our own understanding but on God's. Let's look at Proverbs 3:5–6 in another translation:

Trust in the Lord with all your heart; and lean not to your own understanding. In all your ways acknowledge Him, and He shall direct your paths. (KJVER)

Biblical Hebrew researcher Sarah E. Fisher provides excellent insights on the idea of "leaning" as placing one's trust in something or someone:

Leaning and trust are often found together. It takes a certain amount of trust to lean fully on something. Translators have sometimes replaced *sha'an* (lean/rely) in the Bible with the English word, *trust*. For example, Job's friend, Bildad the Shuhite, understood the simplicity of leaning on the right support, and although most translator[s] use the word *trust* when translating *sha'an*, it actually makes more sense to use the English word *lean*:

Job 8:13b–15

And the hope of the godless will perish, whose confidence is fragile, and whose trust is a spider's web. **He trusts in [leans on: yishaen] his house, but it does not stand**; *he holds fast to it, but it does not endure.*[75]

If we want our lives to be successful, we need to rely entirely on God's wisdom and power every moment of every day, in every situation. Trusting or leaning on our own limited understanding is akin to relying on something as fragile as a spider's web to hold us.

Remember, fear is incited by feelings of being vulnerable, unprotected, and at risk. For most people, when they think that something is more powerful than they are and may affect them adversely, their sense of being in control vanishes. Fear is a powerful force, and, if we are not careful, it will drive us in the wrong direction and impel us to make the wrong decisions. When we make decisions out of a place of either fear or pride, our perspectives become constricted and tainted, something we already battle with due to the sinful nature. Our human understandings cannot bear the total burden of reality, which is why we must lean on God, who alone knows all things and can bear all things. Those who are wise will turn to the Lord

75. Sarah E. Fisher, "Sha'an: Lean on Me," Hebrew Word Lessons, November 29, 2020, https://hebrewwordlessons.com/2020/11/29/shaan-lean-on-me/. Bolding is in the original.

and lean on Him at all times, trusting Him to carry them to a place of peace and strength.

IF WE WANT OUR LIVES TO BE SUCCESSFUL, WE NEED TO RELY ENTIRELY ON GOD'S WISDOM AND POWER EVERY MOMENT OF EVERY DAY, IN EVERY SITUATION.

PRINCIPLE 6: SEEK GOD'S WISDOM

It is easy to fall into anxiety when we need to make an important decision or want to know the right thing to do in a difficult situation. We can dispel our fears by seeking God's wisdom and resting in the assurance that He will provide the guidance we need.

> *If any of you lacks wisdom [to guide him through a decision or circumstance], he is to ask of [our benevolent] God, who gives to everyone generously and without rebuke or blame, and it will be given to him. But he must ask [for wisdom] in faith, without doubting [God's willingness to help], for the one who doubts is like a billowing surge of the sea that is blown about and tossed by the wind. For such a person ought not to think or expect that he will receive anything [at all] from the Lord, being a double-minded man, unstable and restless in all his ways [in everything he thinks, feels, or decides].* (James 1:2–8 AMP)

As we trust in God's faithfulness, leaning on Him, we can ask for His wisdom and expect to receive it, because God is a gracious Giver who supplies everything we need. The double-minded person who vacillates between faith and fear can never have a peaceful, productive life. We must learn to rely wholly on God's perfect wisdom. Let's stop thinking small, because we have a big God who wants to give us the keys to the kingdom. (See Matthew 16:19.) Yet asking for wisdom and having faith that God will answer are essential for activating those keys.

PRINCIPLE 7: SAY THE NAME OF JESUS

As previously described, the name of Jesus has power to save, power to deliver, and power to produce peace during times of trouble. (Remember the story about the elderly woman and the heavenly bulldogs?) Jesus is Savior, He is "God with Us," and His power incorporates all the attributes listed in the Bible in relation to Him, such as "*Wonderful Counselor, Mighty God, Everlasting Father, Prince of Peace*" (Isaiah 9:6 NIV).

The name of Jesus, spoken from a believer's heart or mouth, is a call, an appeal, an invitation for Him to come in all His fullness. When we call on His name, it summons not only His presence but also the Spirit who raised Him from the dead. Jesus's name—invited, welcomed, and celebrated—invokes resurrection power, providing courage, strength, and hope.

PRINCIPLE 8: PRAY CONTINUALLY

In this book, we have discussed various ways in which prayer helps us to overcome fear. Prayer is as essential to your spiritual life as oxygen is to your physical life. A prayer-filled life empowers a fear-free life. Unfortunately, many born-again believers treat prayer like a "fire escape" rather than a daily practice, meaning that they only pray when they are in trouble or need something. That makes as much sense as holding your breath just until you are about to pass out.

An inconsistent prayer life is the reason so many believers find themselves fluctuating in their faith and trust in God, allowing their relationship with Christ to suffer through doubt and fear. They are "up" in faith one day and "down" in fear the next, moving between feeling like they can whip the world and finding themselves beaten, passing out because they were holding their spiritual breaths until their lights went dim.

PRAYER IS AS ESSENTIAL TO YOUR SPIRITUAL LIFE AS OXYGEN IS TO YOUR PHYSICAL LIFE.

In his letter to the church in Thessalonica, Paul, the passionate teacher, admonished the believers regarding the times and seasons in which they were living:

> *For you are all sons of light and sons of day. We do not belong to the night nor to darkness. So then let us not sleep [in spiritual indifference] as the rest [of the world does], but let us keep wide awake [alert and cautious] and let us be sober [self-controlled, calm, and wise]. For those who sleep, sleep at night, and those who are drunk get drunk at night. But since we [believers] belong to the day, let us be sober, having put on the breastplate of faith and love, and as a helmet, the hope and confident assurance of salvation.* (1 Thessalonians 5:5–8 AMP)

In other words, this is no time to be spiritually asleep. You must stay awake, remain sober, and be on fire for God because Satan is like a roaring lion, looking for those he can devour! (See 1 Peter 5:8.)

The dynamic duo of faith and prayer is a winning combination for those seeking to experience freedom from fear. Just as your body is designed to breathe, so your spirit was intended to pray continually! First Thessalonians 5:17 instructs us, "*Pray without ceasing*" (NKJV). The same verse in the *Amplified Bible* reads, "*Be unceasing and persistent in prayer.*" Unceasing prayer indicates a particular urgency to be alert in prayer. So, even when we are not speaking consciously to God, a deep, abiding dependence on Him can be woven into our hearts of faith. In that sense, we "pray" or have the spirit of prayer continuously. Unceasing prayer also implies not giving up on prayer because you have lost faith. Jesus told the parable of the persistent widow to emphasize that His disciples "*should always pray and not give up*" (Luke 18:1 NIV).

The synergy of the Spirit and faith inspires and invigorates your prayers so they are more than hollow words. In the environment of faith, the Spirit mediates our prayers and His responses to them. (See Romans 8:26–27.) If you want the kind of prayer that changes people and circumstances, then you must invite the Holy Spirit to bring everything He is—all He possesses—into the inner courts of your "sanctuary," your being. Then, you will have intimate communion with the Holy Spirit 24/7.

When you enter into this kind of prayer life, you become God's sanctuary; you will never forget the Holy Spirit is with you, because He will never be out of your thoughts. You will entertain His presence, enjoy His fellowship, and celebrate His power and peace every moment of your day.

PRINCIPLE 9: ENFORCE YOUR PEACE

As demonstrated by my encounter with that very determined squirrel whose path I blocked when I was fishing for salmon, the road that leads to true freedom belongs to those brave enough to lay claim to it. We have learned that determination fueled by desperation releases the capacity to defeat or remove anything or anyone that stands between us and all that belongs to our future.

Tackling our fears does take determined courage, but we must always keep in mind that such courage comes from the power of God's voice and presence in our lives. Whatever you think is hindering you from overcoming your fears—whether it is a physical weakness, emotional pain, or anything else—is no match for the courage you can receive from God to rise up in newfound strength, peace, and purpose.

You must also remember to maintain the peace God gives you, staying alert and holding on to God's Word in order to withstand fears that try to bully you into losing your faith and confidence in the Lord. Jesus reigns as the triumphant King, and you can enter into His glorious victory over the enemy, defeating all of his schemes.

PRINCIPLE 10: PRACTICE PRAISE AND WORSHIP

Over the years, I have been a praise and worship leader, a songwriter, and a passionate worshipper of God. Through these experiences, I've discovered something powerful: authentic praise and worship are far more than the sound of rehearsed and performed tunes and lyrics, and they are more profound than the music produced by instruments made of wood, strings, plastic, and metal. Indeed, praise and worship are far more than mere entertainment. The great mystery of how praise and worship reaches the throne of God is finally revealed to us when we realize that *we* are to be the authentic instruments of praise and worship offered to our Lord.

Praise and worship that is permeated with God's power releases a sound that pleases the Lord. When initiated as a response to God's magnificence, our praise and worship is a demonstration of our appreciation of Him as we express our wonder at His love for us! It is a spiritual act of exaltation, adoration, and admiration for our heavenly Father. When we praise God, we thank Him for what He has done, and when we worship Him, we acknowledge Him for who He is in all His greatness.

Our songs penetrate the heavenly realm, and, as God infuses us with His life-giving Spirit, He dispatches supernatural peace and power and releases angelic assistance into our lives. As we humbly stand before the Lord and invite His presence into our midst, every hostile spirit—including the spirit of fear—will scurry for cover.

SCRIPTURES TO STAND ON FOR FEAR-FREE LIVING

Obviously, our lives on earth are never completely free of challenging and even tragic situations. Opposition is a part of the world we live in. Life is a journey, with its ups and downs, triumphs and trials, joys and sorrows. We must decide now how we will respond to these varying circumstances so that we will avoid regressing to our old, fearful ways. Make up your mind that you will not allow fear, but rather the Prince of Peace, to reign in your heart.

I hope you will be inspired and challenged by the following Scriptures I have compiled for living free of fear. Read them now and use them as the basis of your prayers when you rise in the morning, as you progress through the responsibilities and activities of your day, and especially as you prepare to lie down to sleep at night. These passages will energize your faith, quiet your spirit, and fill you with the peace that passes all understanding. (See Philippians 4:6.)

So do not fear, for I am with you; do not be dismayed, for I am your God. I will strengthen you and help you; I will uphold you with my righteous right hand. (Isaiah 41:10 NIV)

When I am afraid, I will put my trust in You. In God, whose word I praise, in God I have put my trust; I shall not be afraid. What can mere mortals do to me? (Psalm 56:3–4 NASB)

Do not be anxious about anything, but in every situation, by prayer and petition, with thanksgiving, present your requests to God. And the peace of God, which transcends all understanding, will guard your hearts and your minds in Christ Jesus. (Philippians 4:6–7 NIV)

Peace I leave with you; my peace I give you. I do not give to you as the world gives. Do not let your hearts be troubled and do not be afraid. (John 14:27 NIV)

God has not given us the spirit of fear; but of power, and of love, and of a sound mind. (2 Timothy 1:7 KJVER)

There is no fear in love. But perfect love drives out fear, because fear has to do with punishment. The one who fears is not made perfect in love. (1 John 4:18 NIV)

When anxiety was great within me, your consolation brought me joy. (Psalm 94:19 NIV)

But now, this is what the Lord says…: "Do not fear, for I have redeemed you; I have summoned you by name; you are mine." (Isaiah 43:1 NASB)

An anxious heart weighs a man down, but a kind word cheers him up. (Proverbs 12:25 NIV84)

Even though I walk through the valley of the shadow of death, I fear no evil, for You are with me; Your rod and Your staff, they comfort me. (Psalm 23:4 NASB)

Have I not commanded you? Be strong and courageous. Do not be terrified; do not be discouraged, for the Lord your God will be with you wherever you go. (Joshua 1:9 NIV84)

Therefore do not worry about tomorrow, for tomorrow will worry about itself. Each day has enough trouble of its own. (Matthew 6:34 NIV)

Therefore humble yourselves under the mighty hand of God [set aside self-righteous pride], so that He may exalt you [to a place of honor in His service] at the appropriate time, casting all your cares [all your anxieties, all your worries, and all your concerns, once and for all] on Him, for He cares about you [with deepest affection, and watches over you very carefully]. (1 Peter 5:6–7 AMP)

Say to those with fearful hearts, "Be strong, and do not fear, for your God is coming to destroy your enemies. He is coming to save you." (Isaiah 35:4 NLT)

Do not worry about your life, what you will eat; or about your body, what you will wear. Life is more than food, and the body more than clothes. Consider the ravens: They do not sow or reap, they have no storeroom or barn; yet God feeds them. And how much more valuable you are than birds! Who of you by worrying can add a single hour to his life? Since you cannot do this very little thing, why do you worry about the rest? (Luke 12:22–26 NIV84)

The Lord is my light and my salvation; whom shall I fear? the Lord is the strength of my life; of whom shall I be afraid? (Psalm 27:1 KJVER)

Cast your cares on the Lord and he will sustain you; he will never let the righteous be shaken. (Psalm 55:22 NIV)

Immediately he spoke to them and said, "Take courage! It is I. Don't be afraid." (Mark 6:50 NIV)

Be strong and courageous. Do not be afraid or terrified because of them, for the Lord your God goes with you; he will never leave you nor forsake you. (Deuteronomy 31:6 NIV)

For I, the Lord your God, hold your right hand; it is I who say to you, "Fear not, I am the one who helps you." Fear not,...I am the one who helps you, declares the Lord; your Redeemer is the Holy One of Israel. (Isaiah 41:13–14 ESV)

God is our refuge and strength, an ever-present help in trouble. (Psalm 46:1 NIV)

The Lord is with me; I will not be afraid. What can mere mortals do to me? The Lord is with me; he is my helper. (Psalm 118:6–7 NIV)

Fear of man will prove to be a snare, but whoever trusts in the Lord is kept safe. (Proverbs 29:25 NIV)

He [Jesus] got up, rebuked the wind and said to the waves, "Quiet! Be still!" Then the wind died down and it was completely calm. He said to his disciples, "Why are you so afraid? Do you still have no faith?" (Mark 4:39–40 NIV)

I sought the LORD, and he answered me; he delivered me from all my fears. Those who look to him are radiant; their faces are never covered with shame. This poor man called, and the LORD heard him; he saved him out of all his troubles. The angel of the LORD encamps around those who fear him, and he delivers them. (Psalm 34:4–7 NIV)

But even if you suffer for doing what is right, God will reward you for it. So don't worry or be afraid of their threats.   (1 Peter 3:14 NLT)

You shall not fear them, for it is the LORD your God who fights for you.   (Deuteronomy 3:22 ESV)

Then he [God] placed his right hand on me and said: "Do not be afraid. I am the First and the Last."   (Revelation 1:17 NIV)

Jesus told him, "Don't be afraid; just believe."   (Mark 5:36 NIV)

I am convinced that nothing can ever separate us from God's love. Neither death nor life, neither angels nor demons, neither our fears for today nor our worries about tomorrow—not even the powers of hell can separate us from God's love.   (Romans 8:38–39 NLT)

The LORD your God is in your midst, a victorious warrior. He will exult over you with joy, He will be quiet in His love, He will rejoice over you with shouts of joy.   (Zephaniah 3:17 NASB)

15

DETERMINATION:
THE LAND OF STICK-TO-ITIVENESS

"If your determination is fixed, I do not counsel you to despair. Few things are impossible to diligence and skill. Great works are performed not by strength, but perseverance."
—Samuel Johnson[76]

I will never forget the look on my mother's face when I breathlessly showed her the bite mark just beneath my left arm.

"What in the world?" she exclaimed. "What happened to your arm?"

Without answering her question directly, I said, "It happened so quickly that I thought it was over!"

"What was over?" she asked.

As I worked to calm my breathing and find the words to explain, I muttered, "The dog, the merry-go-round!"

My mother looked for a clean kitchen cloth and said, "Son, slow down, catch your breath, and tell me exactly what happened."

---

76. "Determination Quotes," LibQuotes, https://libquotes.com/search/?q=determination.

She pulled some ice cubes out of our refrigerator, put them into the cloth, and placed the improvised ice pack where I had been bitten.

By that time, I was ready to continue my story. "Mom, you can't believe what happened to me. Louie's bulldog just bit me!"

She quickly replied, "I can see that, but what exactly happened?"

"I was down the street playing on Louie's new merry-go-round. After a few minutes, Louie's dog, Tugs, started playing with us."

"'Playing'?" she asked. "That doesn't look like Tugs was playing!"

"Mom, he wasn't angry! He was just chasing us around in circles and barking."

"Explain!"

"Well, as we went around in circles, Tugs started following us. It was a game."

"Then what happened?"

Not eager to share the whole story, I said, "We had an idea. Louie threw me Tugs's favorite toy, a rope with a rag tied to the end of it. So, I began to tease Tugs with it. It was the funniest thing! Tugs started running and jumping until, finally, he jumped up and grabbed the rope with his teeth and held on!" I started laughing. "Mom, he wouldn't let go. Sometimes he hung on at least three times around before he let go!"

As my mother applied pressure to the injury on my arm, she began to shake her head. "So you were teasing Tugs?"

"Yes, ma'am!" I replied. "We were just having fun. This dog is amazing! When he grabs hold of something, he doesn't let it go. Especially his favorite toy!"

"You mean Tugs's rope with the rag?"

"Yes, ma'am," I said softly.

As my mother placed more ice on my arm, she asked, "If Tugs was just playing, why is your arm so bruised and bleeding?"

"Mom, you should have seen it! I was swirling around on the merry-go-round and holding the rope out, and the dog jumped up and mistakenly grabbed the skin beneath my arm." I paused for a second, then continued,

"At first, it stung. Then it just got numb! I didn't think anything about it until I felt his weight hanging on me. By the time I realized Tugs was still with me, we were on our second time around! When I looked down to see what was happening, I screamed! Mom, he wasn't letting me go! Tugs thought he was holding on to his toy, but it wasn't his toy—it was my arm. No wonder they call him 'Tugs'! He still wasn't letting me go, so I jumped off the merry-go-round. When Tugs finally let go, he started bouncing around and barking at me because he had just enjoyed the ride on my arm!"

Concluding this wild story, I said, "When I started feeling the pain and saw the blood, I thought it would be better to run home so you could look at where Tugs bit me." I raised my arm away from the ice pack and asked, "I can't see it because it's beneath my arm. Am I okay?"

My mother was working to keep her emotions calm, but she laughed and said, "I think I'll make a phone call to Louie's mother a little later and ask her to keep Tugs and his rag toys in the house next time you are down there playing in their backyard on that merry-go-round!"

Thankfully, I had no broken bones, and Tugs barely broke my skin that day. But while the cuts and bruises soon healed and faded away, the lessons I learned from that small dog stayed with me. In the following days, I realized those bruises on my arm were concrete proof that this dog knew how to hang on to what he believed was his. He was relentless! Once he identified what he wanted, he grabbed it and wouldn't let it go—even if it meant being lifted off the ground and being swung through the air in circles over and over again.

DETERMINATION IS BASED ON INNER STRENGTH

While this story is humorous, I've used it through the years to illustrate the power of inner strength and unyielding determination. I think that, too often, we have allowed the "how" we live to overshadow the "why" for which we live. Because we fail to determine and then remember our chief motivations in life and where we are headed, we lose our way when we are confronted by roadblocks in the form of distractions and difficulties. But those who possess an indomitable "why" for living will always keep on track as they pursue the "how" of life. Our inner strength comes from our why—which, for followers of Jesus, is to love God with all our hearts, love our neighbors as ourselves, make disciples for Jesus, and build His kingdom on earth. (See, for example, Matthew 22:36–40; 28:19; 6:33.) Our internal why determines our external how—the way in which we conduct our lives. And this includes choosing faith over fear.

Martin Luther King Jr. said, "We must constantly build dikes of courage to hold back the flood of fear."[77] Those dikes of courage are created in our inner man by the Spirit. Paul prayed for the Ephesian believers that "[God] *would grant* [them], *according to the riches of His glory, to be strengthened with might by His Spirit in the inner man*" (Ephesians 3:16 KJVER). The Greek word translated *"strengthened"* is *krataioó*, which means "to grow strong," "to prevail by God's dominating strength," and "to attain mastery, the upper hand." This strength "operates by the Lord inworking faith."[78] The Greek word translated *"might"* is *dunamis*, among whose meanings are "force," "ability," "inherent power," and "mighty work."[79]

"Do not fear, for I am with you; do not be afraid, for I am your God. I will strengthen you, I will also help you, I will also uphold you with My righteous right hand" (Isaiah 41:10 NASB). The Spirit's infusion of power in your inner man enriches and invigorates the deepest part of your being, giving you a dominating ability that makes you determined to resist all facets of fear.

"Strength and dignity are her clothing, and she smiles at the future" (Proverbs 31:25 NASB). Although this verse is part of a description of the virtuous woman, it applies to all whose strength is in the Lord. God's empowering presence gives us strength cloaked with a moral force and dignity that arm us against anxiety and worry. This enables us to smile at the future without fearing it as we determine to never give up.

THOSE WHO POSSESS AN INDOMITABLE "WHY" FOR LIVING WILL ALWAYS KEEP ON TRACK AS THEY PURSUE THE "HOW" OF LIFE.

---

77. "Martin Luther King, Jr. Quote," LibQuotes, https://libquotes.com/martin-luther-king-jr/quote/lbk4i9c.
78. *Strong's*, #2901; HELPS Word-studies, #2901, https://biblehub.com/greek/2901.htm.
79. *Strong's*, #1411; Thayer's Greek Lexicon, https://www.bibletools.org/index.cfm/fuseaction/Lexicon.show/ID/G1411/dunamis.htm.

THE POWER OF DETERMINED COMMITMENT

The fact that you've come this far in reading *Fear Must Not Win* tells me that you are not a quitter—you are a finisher! There is no doubt in my mind that you have all it takes to stand against and defeat every fear in your life and to help others overcome and defeat their own fears. Throughout my years of leadership in both the careful examination of God's Word and human behavioral studies, I have found that determined commitment—or "stick-to-itiveness"—is a crucial and creative quality we all need to develop. Those who practice this powerful characteristic find remarkable success in everything they endeavor to do and become. This ability is so notable that it has been practiced and promoted by the world's most successful authors, thinkers, visionaries, and entrepreneurs.

It takes determination to see our hopes come to pass. The question is not "Will you begin?" but "Will you finish?" The most glorious pages of human history belong to those who were relentless and fearless in their single-minded pursuit of their objectives, regardless of the costs. Consider the unwavering determination and uncompromising tenacity that characterized such individuals as Moses, David, the Lord Jesus Christ, the apostle Paul, Martin Luther, John Wesley, Harriet Tubman, Gladys Aylward, Martin Luther King Jr., Mother Teresa, and Nelson Mandela. Each of these individuals either found a way or made a way to do what they were called to do. If you don't possess the power of determination and a true commitment to your life's mission, even if you had all the courage in the world, it would be without consequence.

Richard DeVos, a billionaire who was the founder of Amway and the owner of the Orlando Magic basketball team, said, "If I had to select one quality, one personal characteristic that I regard as being most highly correlated with success, whatever the field, I would pick the trait of persistence. Determination. The will to endure to the end, to get knocked down seventy times and get up off the floor saying, 'Here comes number seventy-one!'"[80]

Vince Lombardi Jr. once said, "A man can be as great as he wants to be. If you believe in yourself and have the courage, the determination, the dedication, the competitive drive and if you are willing to sacrifice the little

---

80. "Richard DeVos Quotes," AZ Quotes, https://www.azquotes.com/quote/536979.

things in life and pay the price for the things that are worthwhile, it can be done."[81] It is this type of determined commitment that will lead you to embrace a fearless life so you can fulfill your purpose, which is attainable through the power of God's Spirit as you cooperate with Him.

It has been said that you don't lose until you quit. I also think that you cannot lose *unless* you quit! Grant Cardone, who is a successful author and real-estate mega-life coach, says, "All difficulties can be overcome by the right amount of effort (requires commitment and persistence).... No commitment equals no results."[82] Cardone is known for the "10X rule," a philosophy that holds, "One of the major differences between successful and unsuccessful people is that the former look for problems to resolve, whereas the latter make every attempt to avoid them."[83] Most people fear the thought of the worst-case scenario, but if the worst-case scenario becomes reality, they can often handle themselves quite well. Fear of failure holds us back more than the failure itself.

Those who dare to understand the power of commitment and who practice incorporating determination into their lives become rich—in the fullest sense of that word. This power pays dividends in every area of your life. If you don't believe that stick-to-itiveness is necessary, remember the following, which we discussed earlier: unless we exercise a righteous stubbornness, the peace we have attained by God's strength can easily slip away.

God wants to do great things in our lives. And when we set lofty goals and dreams of what could be, based on God's Word and the Spirit's leading, we will be challenged by the process of attaining these visions of the future. Raw grit, combined with faith and a reliance on God's strength, will be required if we are to succeed.

Do not, therefore, fling away your [fearless] confidence, for it has a glorious and great reward.   (Hebrew 10:35 AMP)

---

81. "Vince Lombardi Jr. Quotes," Goodreads, https://www.goodreads.com/quotes/6546139-a-man-can-be-as-great-as-he-wants-to.

82. "Grant Cardone on Persistence and Commitment," Cardone Solutions, https://cardonesolutions.com/persistence-and-commitment/.

83. "Grant Cardone Quotes," Goodreads, https://www.goodreads.com/author/quotes/1638887.Grant_Cardone.

THE QUESTION IS NOT "WILL YOU BEGIN?" BUT "WILL YOU FINISH?"

COUNTING THE COST

One significant way in which we develop determined commitment is by acknowledging and accepting the cost of following Jesus. In Luke 14, we see that, as Jesus's ministry grew and He became more well-known, the crowds gathered around Him wherever He went. But the motives of the plethora of people surrounding Him were not always pure. Many of them were not seeking God but rather things like free food and miracles, and Jesus knew their hearts. They loved the advantages of being associated with Jesus but didn't want to pay a price for that association.

Other religious leaders might enjoy building huge "platforms" to their advantage, but not Jesus. He was on a different course, one with a divine purpose. He wanted to create a company of disciples that would change the world. Therefore, to make clear to people what it really means to be His disciple, Jesus explained the condition. The condition He shared would rock people's boats because even those who were closest to Him enjoyed the notoriety of being connected with Him. *"If anyone comes to Me and does not hate his father and mother, wife and children, brothers and sisters, yes, and his own life also, he cannot be My disciple. And whoever does not bear his cross and come after Me cannot be My disciple"* (Luke 14:26–27 NKJV). To be clear, Jesus was not suggesting that we turn our backs on those we love. He was saying that if we truly want to be His disciples, we must make the decision to place Him first above all others, including ourselves. Self-denial is the first lesson in the school of discipleship, and, for Jesus, it is the indispensable condition of following Him.

Those who are not willing to patiently undergo trials, afflictions, and persecutions for the sake of Christ and the kingdom of God are not worthy to be Jesus's disciples. If you choose to be a disciple, you will pay the cost of following Him. You must count the cost and learn to maintain your peace, even when you face trials and persecutions.

For which of you, intending to build a tower, does not sit down first and count the cost, whether he has enough to finish it…? Or what king, going to make war against another king, does not sit down first and consider whether he is able with ten thousand to meet him who comes against him with twenty thousand? (Luke 14:28, 30–31 NKJV)

After setting up the requirement for being a disciple, Jesus asked His would-be followers some questions, which was one of His styles of communication. I've often wondered if the disciples understood the premise of Jesus's questions here. As I like to say, there is power in a question. A question is an answer in seed form. In His second question, Jesus used the analogy of kings, which could be applied to anyone who possesses authority.

These two provocative questions about determining if you have the resources to build a tower or to wage war were meant to make the listeners think about the application to their own lives in terms of being disciples of Jesus. The questions were the springboard for Jesus's concluding points:

So likewise, whoever of you does not forsake all that he has cannot be My disciple. Salt is good; but if the salt has lost its flavor, how shall it be seasoned? It is neither fit for the land nor for the dunghill, but men throw it out. He who has ears to hear, let him hear! (Luke 14:33–35 NKJV)

Jesus was asking the crowds if they had the courage and passion to finish the race. He teaches us that once we have chosen to follow Him, we should always guard this commitment. We should calculate the cost and then lay the foundation required to follow Him. That is why we must continuously walk in step with the Spirit, who will stir within us the zeal required to finish the race, regardless of the trials and temptations that come our way. We need supernatural fervor and endurance to stay strong in our faith.

WE MUST COUNT THE COST AND LEARN TO MAINTAIN OUR PEACE, EVEN WHEN WE FACE TRIALS AND PERSECUTIONS.

Compared to believers who live in countries where there is constant and/or severe persecution, Christians in the United States are spiritually wealthy. Even with all of its challenges, our nation still offers us the greatest freedoms and opportunities in the world. Many people who live under oppressive governments or closed societies cannot attend church, worship or pray publicly, or own a Bible. Yet they are willing to risk everything they have, including their own lives, for the sake of Christ! We are blessed to have tens of thousands of churches in which we can freely worship God and hear His Word; an abundance of Bibles in various translations; a wealth of Bible commentaries; Christian television programs and networks; and other resources. There are close to a hundred and fifty Christian universities and colleges that we can attend in person or online. And there are numerous Christian organizations that serve a variety of spiritual and material needs we may have. And yet, millions of American believers appear to be spiritually powerless and unprepared because they are unwilling to pay the price required to follow Christ. While salvation is free, commitment is costly.

Having authentic, lasting peace requires a willingness to give God everything and the commitment to follow Him at any cost. As we make the decision to keep Him first in all our ways, His presence fills our lives. We become living tabernacles of His purpose, peace, and power. We are like the builder of the tower Jesus spoke about in Luke 14. We need to count the cost of what it takes to build our lives in Him. We are to be towers of strength and courage where the Holy Spirit abides. (See Ephesians 6:10.) We are to be *a city set on a hill* (Matthew 5:14, various translations).

FREEDOM REQUIRES PERSISTENCE

Remember Jesus's warning to Peter in the garden of Gethsemane about his need for a determined commitment? He admonished Peter to *"watch and pray"* so that he would not fall into temptation and stray from faithfully following Jesus.

And He [Jesus] went a little further, and fell on His face, and prayed, saying, O My Father, if it be possible, let this cup pass from Me: nevertheless not as I will, but as You will. And He comes to the

disciples, and finds them asleep, and says to Peter, What, could you not watch with Me one hour? Watch and pray, that you enter not into temptation: the Spirit indeed is willing, but the flesh is weak.
(Matthew 26:39–41 KJVER)

Interestingly, while Peter and the other disciples who were with him were yielding to the temptation to fall asleep, Jesus was actively wrestling with the powers of darkness over the salvation of souls. Thankfully, all creation would soon witness the power of Jesus's unswerving love in the form of His tenacity to finish what He came to earth to accomplish.

One of the most famous portions of poetry in all of T. S. Eliot's poetic works is the fifth and concluding section of "The Hollow Men," which contains these legendary lines:

Between the idea

And the reality...

Falls the Shadow[84]

We could say that between the cross and the resurrection falls the shadow. But the shadow is lifted when we hear Jesus cry, *"It is finished!"* (John 29:30, various translations), and when we hear the angel say, *"He is not here; he has risen!"* (Luke 24:6 NIV).

Every fallen angel who bet against Jesus's ability to fulfill His mission shook in alarm when they heard those words! Jesus accomplished within thirty-three short years what no one else—not even the greatest men and women of history—could do in all their years: secure our salvation, healing, and peace for eternity! How did He do this? *He refused to let go of us.* Our peace required His persistence. Thank God, Jesus didn't quit!

Because of the joy awaiting him, he endured the cross, disregarding its shame. Now he is seated in the place of honor beside God's throne. Think of all the hostility he endured from sinful people; then you won't become weary and give up.   (Hebrews 12:2–3 NLT)

The apostle Paul found himself at points of frustration, weariness, and physical danger during the low moments of his ministry. Yet he always

---

84. T. S. Eliot, "The Hollow Men," All Poetry, https://allpoetry.com/the-hollow-men.

rebounded, determined to finish the race. (See 2 Timothy 4:7.) The Scriptures urge us to make the same choice of determined commitment:

> Let us strip off every weight that slows us down, especially the sin that so easily trips us up. And let us run with endurance the race God has set before us. We do this by keeping our eyes on Jesus, the champion who initiates and perfects our faith. (Hebrews 12:1–2 NLT)

Be encouraged! The testing of your faith is meant to produce perseverance in you so you can develop into a mature, fear-free person. (See James 1:2–4.) Yes, there will be times of trouble, but God will use even your fear to cultivate your faith to maturity. To the natural, unspiritual mind, such a concept seems foreign. But for the trained child of God and spiritual warrior who is led by God's Spirit, joy and sorrow, acceptance and rejection, peace and disruptions go hand in hand.

We have the stuff of which martyrs are made, in the fullest sense of that word, which, in the Greek, means "witness." "Bearing witness" is a legal concept, and as children of the Most High God, we present the gospel without fear of preaching the crucified Christ, who died to save the world. We bear witness to the role Christ plays in our lives as we live out our faith daily. Our holy response to life's difficulties—disagreements, problems, grievances, strife, pain, suffering, tribulation, and failure—is manifested in how we address our fears and anxieties.

As I said earlier, we might bend, but we will not be broken! Even if we are surrounded on every hand, we can remember what Elisha said to his servant: "Don't be afraid…. Those who are with us are more than those who are with them" (2 Kings 6:16 NIV).

People are often surprised to hear me say things like "I don't do fear anymore!" "I don't do intimidation any longer!" or "I don't do depression anymore!" But once they understand what is behind these expressions, they often want to pursue a fear-free life too. God designed you to win, not lose! And, again, winning over fear or any other obstacle requires righteous determination, tenacity, stubbornness, and stick-to-itiveness.

We must realize that our transformation from being fearful to becoming free of fear is not automatic. Sufferings do not inevitably remodel us. Our positive or negative response to adversity determines whether it will help us or hurt us. *Resilience* means responding well to adversity so that we can withstand it and recover from our difficulties. God's grace is the key that enables us to respond well when times are tough. Helen Keller showed that she understood how to overcome life's disadvantages when she said, "Although the world is full of suffering, it is full also of the overcoming of it. My optimism, then, does not rest on the absence of evil, but on a glad belief in the preponderance of good and a willing effort always to cooperate with the good, that it may prevail."[85]

THE IMPORTANCE OF THIS MOMENT

As we come to the end of this book, I can sense both the power and the necessity of this moment. I want to challenge you to make a personal commitment that you will never surrender the peace and power you have discovered. Don't allow the peace God gave you to be stolen or forfeited. Remember the words of 2 Timothy 1:7: *"God has not given us the spirit of fear; but of power, and of love, and of a sound mind"* (KJVER). By committing to fear-free living, right here and now, you resolve in your heart to not only apprehend but also hold tightly to the principles I've shared with you. In this moment, make up your mind that you will never again allow fear to reign in your heart!

I also challenge you to offer what God has given you to the people around you. I pray that, by now, there remains no doubt in your mind that you have all it takes to not only stand against and defeat every fear in your life but also help others to overcome and defeat their fears. Tell people how you found God's peace and power and how you maintain these qualities in your life. Perhaps a family member or friend is struggling with fear. Pray about sharing this book with them. Whatever area you work in—whether you are a business owner, a professional athlete, an artist, an engineer, a real estate agent, a homemaker, or another profession—consider sharing this book with the people around you. The truths and principles will assist them to overcome their fears and become the courageous models of success God designed them to be. If you've

---

85. "Helen Keller Quotes," https://www.goodreads.com/quotes/818488-although-the-world-is-full-of-suffering-it-is-full.

been blessed, share, share, share! As you do, you will be amazed by the ways in which it will come back to you over and over again.

God has equipped you and called you for such a time as this. (See Esther 4:14.) You must not shrink back—seize the moment! This is your time. Spread the word! You have the power to face your fears, kill those giants, and live a fear-free life.

Fear must not win!

MY CLOSING PRAYER AND DECLARATION FOR YOU

Father, I thank You for my new friend. I ask that, in the days ahead, You would breathe new life into their whole being. I declare that worry, anxiety, and everything else related to fear would have no more power over them. Your Son, Jesus, paid the eternal price to defeat sin, sickness, death, and disease. He bore the cost not only for our sins but also for our healing and our peace. Father God, I ask that, from this moment, You would place a divine assurance of Your love in the heart of my friend, and that nothing will be able to stand against them all the days of their life. I pray that, even in those difficult moments when the challenges seem greatest, You would awaken Your power within their spirit! I declare and agree together with them that You are greater than anything they might face in life. In Your presence, they will find peace and power, and they will always remain in Your care. In Jesus's name, amen!

ABOUT THE AUTHOR

Mark Steven Filkey is the founder and senior pastor of WestCoast World Outreach Church, a multicultural, interdenominational ministry located in the beautiful delta city of Stockton, California. He also oversees a large number of churches across the United States and around the world.

Mark is a gifted author praise and worship leader, songwriter, musician, recording artist, producer, motivational speaker, philanthropist, life coach, and mentor to many. With a unique mixture of teaching, music, and humor, he has a gift of bridging cultural and denominational divides and of igniting fresh levels of faith, love, and revelation in the hearts of his audiences everywhere.

Mark and his wife, Jordana, are well-respected pastors, international conference speakers, and psalmists. They are known for their heart toward others and their ability to pour into leaders and their families personally and prophetically with acute spiritual accuracy. Mark and Jordana have four sons: Jake, Jordan, Joel, and Jael.

Mark Steven Filkey
PO Box 1966
Lodi, California, 95241
www.MarkFilkey.com
(Download the free WestCoast Church super app.)